"*NUTS!*"

A 101ST AIRBORNE DIVISION
MACHINE GUNNER AT BASTOGNE

"NUTS!"

A 101ST AIRBORNE DIVISION
MACHINE GUNNER AT BASTOGNE

VINCENT J. SPERANZA

DEEDS PUBLISHING | ATLANTA

Printed in the United States of America

Cover photograph © Eddy Bertels – used by permission

Cover design by Mark Babcock and Matt King

Published by Deeds Publishing, Marietta, GA
www.deedspublishing.com

Library of Congress Cataloging-in-Publications Data is available on request.

ISBN 978-1-941165-51-5

Books are available in quantity for promotional or premium use. For information, write Deeds Publishing, PO Box 682212, Marietta, GA 30068 or info@deedspublishing.com.

First edition, 2014

10 9 8 7 6 5 4 3 2 1

AUTHOR'S NOTE

PLEASE NOTE THAT I HAVE MADE NO ATTEMPT AT SERIOUS RESEARCH FOR this project. I do not have the inventive genius of a writer. I am only a story teller. This is merely the story of my life as I lived it, and as I remember it. —VJS

CONTENTS

ACKNOWLEDGMENTS

AMONG THE MYRIAD INFLUENCES THAT HAVE SHAPED MY LIFE AND THIS story, I am most grateful to family, friends, acquaintances and passersby who, through their kindness, support and humanity have added so much to my journey.

Dr. Albert Speranza who has inspired so many of us.

My wife and life-long partner, Iva, without whom I could not have lived this life so well.

My children: daughter, Kathy, trip organizer, travel companion and all around administrative assistant and my son, Vinnie, keeper of the home fires and supporter extraordinaire.

My entire extended family for their continued love and support.

Bob and Mark Babcock of Deeds Publishing, who made my memoirs a living reality.

Monsieur Eddy Bertels for his excellent photograph used for the front cover and his loyal friendship.

Senator Fred Thompson for his kindness and comments.

Special Thanks to General H. L. Altshuler, my new "Fox Hole" buddy without whose dedicated and inspired help, this book would have remained mired in technical difficulties. Thanks again Buz.

To all the guys buried under white markers all across the globe

INTRODUCTION

THIS IS THE STORY OF ONE MEMBER OF AMERICA'S GREATEST GENERATION as told by the author in his warm, humoristic style that draws you into his world and takes you along his life journey. From his childhood as a first generation American growing up in a close-knit Italian family on New York's Staten Island to coming of age on the battlefields of World War II Europe, from Bastogne to Berchtesgaden, and maturing in post-war America as a combat veteran in pursuit of the American Dream, Vince Speranza shares his life adventure with humor, emotion, and candor.

Having grown up in the rural environment that was Staten Island in the late twenties and thirties, he graduated from high school and joined the Army at eighteen. There was a war on and Vince wanted to defend his beloved country. An Infantryman, he became a paratrooper and joined the 101st Airborne Division just before the Battle of the Bulge. Dug in on the outskirts of Bastogne during that bitterly cold and seemingly interminable period of continuous tank and artillery bombardment, Vince and his fellow paratroopers held their ground and stopped Adolf Hitler's last violent attempt to delay or reverse his inevitable defeat before it reached the town.

He describes his very clear and accurate recollections of his unit's actions against an overwhelmingly numerically superior force during the Battle for Bastogne, and recalls modestly his role in the founding of a very special Belgian lager now known throughout Belgium and Luxembourg as Airborne Beer; a role that has made him a modern day celebrity to pub owners and beer drinkers across the region.

He describes his recuperation from wounds received in direct contact with the retreating enemy in Belgium, the kindness and compassion showed by hospital staff and ordinary citizens in England and the circuitous route he took to insure he would rejoin his old unit upon his return to duty. Then there is the fight across the Rhine, the liberation of concentration camps, and the search and clearing of the Eagles' Nest, Hitler's famous mountain retreat in Berchtesgaden; the stand down of the 101st and a period of occupation duty before the long awaited return home and discharge to begin another completely different set of adventures.

There is a fascinating stint in the Merchant Marine, a series of low level jobs while earning his college degree, a heartwarming courtship, a lasting marriage, three great kids, and highly successful careers in both education and labor relations.

This is Vince Speranza's "Story of My Life and How I Lived It." It is a human interest story, a piece of the history of an era that changed the world, written in the first person by a man who lived it. If you don't know anyone from the Greatest Generation or have never spoken to any of them, you need to read this book.

—H. L. Buz Altshuler, Major General, U.S. Army, Retired

1. MY FATHER COMES
TO AMERICA

IN A SMALL MOUNTAIN VILLAGE IN PALMI, REGGIO CALABRIA, JUST across the Straits of Messina from Sicily, Francesco Rafaello Speranza speaks to his family. His wife, Francesca, and all of the kids, Rocco, Joey, Nunciata, Concetta, Patsy, and little Frankie stood with frowns on their faces.

"We are going to America" says my grandfather. The kids suck in their breaths. "But not to stay," announces their father. "We will be there five years and everyone will go to work every day, even little Frankie, and every penny will be saved. We will then have enough money to buy a piece of land here in Palmi and build a house on it. The Speranza family will be landowners.

"The kids suck in their breaths again, only this time with a smile on their faces; already anxious to run outdoors and tell all of their friends how they are going to America.

And so they did.

Five years later, at a dock in lower Manhattan, a passenger ship heading for Palermo, Sicily is being loaded. Once more young Frankie and Patsy plead with their father to stay in America.

"Papa it is so nice here. We can get good jobs and go to school."

"The family is going back to Italy, understand?"

The ship's angry horn announces its impatience to leave. People on shore give their last waves and the people aboard ship, some laughing, some crying, wave back. The large hawsers attaching the ship to the dock are being cast off. Just as the gangplank is being removed, two small boys, Frankie and his brother Patsy, rush down the gangplank and disappear into the crowd on the docks.

My father had come to America to stay.

Can you imagine two small boys, aged 13 and 15, with nothing but the shirts on their backs, on their own in New York City? They went to the Catholic Church in lower Manhattan and asked the priest for something to eat and a place to stay for the night; that they would leave first thing in the morning to look for a job.

The next morning they went down to the docks and found that a ship was in need of two cabin boys. The ship was going to California and the boys were delighted because they knew that everybody in California got rich with gold. It was to sail from New York to Panama (the canal had not yet been built) and then passengers traveled overland to another ship going to San Francisco.

However, my father told me, the voyage was a nightmare. His older brother, Patsy, was in a fight every day to keep predators away who wished to use cabin boys in other ways. They decided to jump ship as soon as it reached Panama. In Panama, penniless because jumping ship meant they did not get paid, they got a job at a frankfurter stand. "A very good job," said my father, "Good pay, and plenty to eat. When we had enough money, we boarded a ship back to New York."

Now what! In the next few years these boys took every available opportunity to make a dollar. They shined shoes, delivered groceries, ran errands, sold newspapers, and moved from living on the streets to a room above a candy store on Delancy Street. At age 15 my father and his brother Patsy, 17, were recruited for the coal mines in West Virginia. They were told that transportation would be free, a place to live would be provided, and they would receive good pay. They were *not* told that they would be paid in script—not dollars. It also meant that even before starting work they were in debt to the Company for food and lodging. All of the bosses were Irish who, at that time, were one generation ahead of the Italians, and never let them forget it. The Italians were called Wops and Guinies and all sorts of derogatory names. When they asked for more heavy posts to prop up the mine roof, they were told, "Wops are cheaper than props." When my father could stand it no longer, they left.

"How did you get away, Pop?" I asked.

"I hit the boss in the head with a shovel, and Patsy and I ran to the highway. We never looked back. We had nothing in the way of money, so we hitchhiked north. We stopped at little towns, got some temporary work, fed and clothed ourselves, and got back to New York."

At age 16, my father was able to take the test for a chauffeur's license in New York City. He says he then made out very well doing private chauffeuring work for wealthy individuals. He never would admit it outright but, he did say that several of the "clients" were extremely well-dressed, good tippers, but real tough looking. The Black Hand (forerunner of the Mafia) ruled the NYC streets in those days.

His chauffeur work required him to be well groomed, so he frequented the barbershop on Mulberry Street. Barbershops in those days were more than just for haircuts. They were centers of political activity, local news and gossip, medical treatment (some barbershops even pulled teeth), and social centers. It was there that Pop met Mom.

He went for a haircut one day and said that he could see past the curtain in the doorway in back of the shop where the family lived. And here was this pretty little sixteen year old girl, twirling, dancing, and flinging her hips, (my mother would always blush when Pop told the story). He said she did it to attract his attention; she said she never thought anyone was looking.

Pop is now in a quandary; he knows he needs to ask the barber, Don Vincenzo, for permission to call on his daughter, but how to admit that he saw her through the curtains at the back of the barbershop. It must have been resolved somehow because when she was seventeen, they married. Within the first year came Joey, two years later Nancy, two years later Frances, and in 1925, Vincent. There would be four more children later.

At the time I was born, the family lived on Delancy Street, Hell's Kitchen it was called, and a real tough neighborhood. My mother stood it until 1928. When my brother, Joey, got hit in the head with a milk bottle (made of heavy glass in those days) in a street fight, Mom got real angry. He required serious medical attention and Mom had had it. She told my father that they needed to move. She also told him that her mother had a house on Staten Island with empty rooms upstairs and would welcome them if they wanted to move there.

The problem was that, by this time, Pop had gotten a steady job with R.H. Macy and Company as a warehouse maintenance man (janitor), but it was in Flushing Meadows, Queens. To get to work from Staten Island, Pop would have to take two buses, the Staten Island Ferry, and then the subway from South Ferry, through Manhattan, through the Bronx, through Queens, and up to Flushing Meadows. That was a two and a half hour trip, including time to change clothes to be ready for work.

Reluctantly, my father agreed and the family moved to Staten Island.

The only recollection I have of the Delancy Street apartment was my father coming home from work and handing me the newspaper. Being three years old at the time, I did not know what to do with it but I knew that if I held it, the next thing out of his pocket was a little piece of chocolate called Suchard, available for a penny at machines in all of the subways.

I recall for the longest time that the youngest child who greeted Pop at the door always got a piece of Suchard chocolate.

2. GROWING UP ON STATEN ISLAND

STATEN ISLAND IS ONE OF THE FIVE BOROUGHS OF NEW YORK CITY. IT IS 7 x 13 miles (width and length) and today has over one million people on it. Actually it's much closer to the state of New Jersey. It is separated from it by just a narrow body of water called the Kill van Kull and there are three bridges connecting it to New Jersey. It is a large bay away from the rest of New York City.

Until 1964 when the Verrazano Narrows Bridge was built, the only communication with the rest of the city was the Staten Island ferry, a 25 minute ride from St. George Staten Island to lower Manhattan. The history of the Island goes back to when the British owned New York City. The Royal Navy forbade all development on Staten Island because the Island had a magnificent growth of tall sturdy oak trees necessary for the masts of the ships of the Royal Navy.

When the colonies declared their independence from Britain, New York State and New Jersey both claimed Staten Island. It was decided to settle the matter with a sailboat race around the Island. New York settled on Captain Billip, its best captain, and New Jersey selected its best captain and ship. Captain Billip won the race for New York (there is a monument to him on Staten Island, on the South Shore) and the island became officially a part of New York State and the city.

Because of its location, it lagged behind the development of New York City and was considered one of the outlying areas. In fact, punishment for errant policemen in New York City was meted out by assigning the man to a patrol on Staten Island, "out in the sticks."

I mention this because, although I grew up in New York City, I really had a semi-rural upbringing. While I was growing up on Staten Island, unlike the rest of the city, there were more horses and wagons than automobiles, and only the main roads were paved. Woods and streams abounded.

My first recollection on Staten Island, I was three years old at the time, was seeing the moving truck bringing our household goods from Delancey Street actually drive across a field to get to our home (my grandmother's house) which I thought was strange.

The road did not go directly to my grandmother's house. The address of that house was 584 Villa Avenue. It had a full-length basement, three large railroad rooms (three in-line) downstairs, and three large railroad rooms upstairs. My grandmother occupied the downstairs and seven Speranzas occupied the upstairs.

For the first couple of years, the bedroom was occupied by my parents and the youngest baby, my two sisters slept on the folding couch in the living room. My two brothers and I had a folding bed in the kitchen. It meant we could not go to bed until all the company left the house as the kitchen was the general meeting room for all occasions. How I remember my brothers and me slouching against the wall, sleepy, waiting for everybody to go home so we could go to bed. The only time we remained alert and listening to the adult conversation was when Grandma was telling stories.

My grandmother was the most fantastic storyteller in the world. She spoke only in Italian and, at the time, most of us knew enough of the language to understand her. When Grandma told a story, every adult in the room was absolutely still and all eyes focused on her, listening intently, immediately prepared to laugh or cry depending on the story grandma was telling. Because we weren't sitting at the table, we children would crane our necks toward Grandma, trying to catch every word.

She told a series of stories about a seemingly idiot boy named Giova, who always managed, very cleverly, to save the day. How we loved those stories. I can still remember one or two of them today, but they have to be told in Italian.

It wasn't until I was about age eight that the family finally put together enough money to finish the upstairs attic rooms which were just as large as the downstairs rooms and so provided plenty of space for growing children.

In the outside world, Staten Island had all kinds of fascinating things to do. First of all there was a brook alongside the house. Tiny fish, frogs, snakes, darning needles (dragon flies), and all other kinds of interesting critters kept us very busy during spring and summer.

By age eight, all boys were allowed to have a pocket knife. That pocket knife was used for everything from peeling an apple (you ate the peelings; you didn't throw them away), to playing mumbley peg, and shaping, carving, and whittling all kinds of wood.

One of the basic raw materials for a lot of our "inventions" was the wooden house-shingle. The things we learned to make included a "plop-plop boat." The plop-plop boat was made by placing your knife at about four inches at the thick end of the shingle and then whacking it so that you now had a piece of shingle four inches wide and about eighteen inches long. You then sharpened the thick end of the shingle to a point which became the bow of the boat. Next you cut out about three inches off the back end (thin part) of the shingle, leaving a half inch on each side.

That left an open space in the back of the boat where you put a rubber band. Using the piece of shingle you cut out, you made a small lever which was then stuck into the rubber band. When wound up, it would "plop plop" the boat across the water. Oh, the races we had with those boats and the frustration when the boats would not go straight because you didn't carve the point right, or when you would wind the prop too tight and broke the rubber band, or the countless impediments in the brook which knocked the boat off course.

Probably one of the worst "crimes" ever perpetrated against young boys was the invention of the tubeless tire. It meant that the automobile tire no longer had an inner tube which, when discarded, was the basis for all kinds of imaginative implements. A band about a half-inch wide cut from a rubber tube was the power for the shingle-arrow. Very simply, you took your trusty knife and cut a one inch strip of shingle. Then about three inches down from the thin edge, you began carving on both sides until you had an arrow with the thinnest portion being the "feather" and the sharpened thick end, the point.

With an inner tube rubber band doubled over your left hand, you placed the shingle-arrow in the band, drew back, and fired. Never, of course, at each other but up and down the brook there were lots of targets. What contests we had. Whenever there was a frog visible, you would see if you could pin him to the mud with an arrow.

By today's standards I imagine people would have considered us cruel to animals, but that was a different era.

Another thing we had a lot of fun with was the rubber band gun. You cut about a 15 inch piece of 2 x 4 and drove a big nail three inches from one end. Split one of your mother's wooden clothes pins in half and held it to the 2x4 with two thick rubber bands. The nail acted as a trigger hold so when you pulled on it the clothes pin would open and close against the 2 x 4. Holding it open, you stuck one end of another rubber band in the gun and stretched it out to and over the end. A squeeze on the trigger and the rubber band would fly. We could shoot at each other with that weapon because it was non-lethal. We chased each other around the field with rubber band guns for many an hour.

And then there were the seasonal activities. At about age ten, we were allowed the more dangerous things, for example, slingshots. We went out into the woods looking for the proper fork of a tree branch, cut it off, and went home to skin it. The next time the oven was lit, your mother would allow you to "bake" the green branch. When it came out, it was hard and fit for a proper slingshot. Using tire-tube rubber bands and spaghetti string you tied two long rubbers to the fork. Then you went looking for an old shoe and cut out the tongue, squared off a piece of it, put two slits in it, and tied the rubber bands to those slits to form the pouch. You are now ready for action, hunting along the brook.

Of course you need ammunition. Woe to the people in the neighborhood who had those white pebble driveways because the white pebbles were perfect slingshot ammo. We would raid the place at night, fill our pockets with the pebbles, and the next day we could go up and down the brook. This time the targets were a little more challenging than a stationary frog. We prided ourselves on seeing if we could hit dragonflies. The dragonflies would fly up and down the brook and land on a stone or the weeds that grew at the water's edge. If you were lucky enough or skillful enough to get one, you carried it around all day to show off your prowess.

In the spring there was also a certain reed that grew along the edges of the brook. It was about 1/2 inch in diameter and if cut at a length of 12 inches and allowed to dry, made a perfect hollow tube. We called them "putty blowers" or bean shooters. The ammunition for these putty blowers was the early buds of the wild cherry tree. There were a lot of wild cherry trees in the woods near our house.

At a certain period of their growth, we climbed the trees, stripped pods of the little green future cherries, and then painstakingly sat down and pulled off all the little stems. When they dried, they were almost perfectly round ammo for our bean shooters. You put a handful in your mouth and then proceeded to blow them out through the tube. Sometimes we took them to school. If you got caught with one in school, the teachers played havoc with your knuckles. In those days teachers were allowed to punish students with their 12 inch oak rulers (a boy on his knuckles and a girl on the open hand).

Most families during the Great Depression had a pet dog, but it was strictly for utilitarian purposes. It remained chained to the dog-house outside and it's only function was to bark when anyone came near. So you might say there were no personal pet dogs. But we boys found ways to bring other pets into our world, starting with snakes. We had been told as children that there were no poisonous snakes on Staten Island, so we did not have to worry about capturing a snake. Around the brook and in the fields there were lots of garter snakes and every boy had one in his pocket. Those who dared brought them to school and scared the daylights out of the more squeamish boys and all the girls. But again, if you got caught, punishment was swift.

There was a certain kind of toad that made a good pet. It remained very quietly in your pocket so you didn't have to worry about it crawling out like the snakes did. When you put it out on your desk, it croaked. It was a gurgling sounding croak which even the girls liked. Whenever the teacher left the room, putting a student monitor in charge, we would have croaking contests to determine whose toad could croak the loudest and whose had the prettiest voice. We seldom had a chance to really vote on it though; the teacher always came back too soon.

Then there were the singing locusts, Lokis we called them. Only in certain years would they come out but, when they did, it was just grand. You would listen to the locusts' song, trace it to the tree, wait for him to start singing again (they said when he sings, he's blind) and grab him. Then you "borrowed" a spool of thread from your mother's sewing box, tied it to one of his 10 or 12 legs, put a pencil in the spool, and turned him loose. Now you had your own little flying kite Loki. You proudly walked around flying a Loki up there as if he were a pedigree dog on a stroll. After a certain amount of time the locust would get tired and come to the ground. That's when you knew you had to turn him loose and go find another.

When you were about ten or older, you were allowed to go "play" a little further from the neighborhood, with due notice to your older brother who was responsible for you. At a distance from the house there was a pond called Willowbrook. It had lots of fish in it, so we were told. That summer, five of us from our neighborhood (strength in numbers) decided to go fishing in Willowbrook Pond. We dug up some worms. Nobody had money for fishhooks or fishing poles so we just went out to the woods, looked for a nice long willow tree branch, had spaghetti string from home for fishline, and a bent pin for a hook. It's really tough to catch fish with bent pins since they had no barb on them, but if as soon as the fish bit you jerked it hard up in the air, the bent pin would hold the fish long enough for it to go sailing up over your head and onto the grass. We didn't catch a lot of fish but we had a lot of fun.

By now you are probably asking, "What in the hell is spaghetti string?" Well, whenever we went to the grocery store to buy pasta (spaghetti) loose from big storage drawers, Mrs. Perricone wrapped it in white paper and tied it with string which we kids saved for later use. Spaghetti string. "Capice?"

On some summer evenings we would have the Van Riper Street Gang versus the Villa Avenue Gang and Indian raids like you never saw before. You "borrowed" your parents' garbage can lid for your shield. You had a stick about three feet long for your sword which went in your belt, and then you had your spear. The spear was a certain weed that grew in our fields which, when dried, was so light weight you couldn't hurt a flea with it. It looked like cotton wool material inside. We never knew what the thing was but when you stripped all the little side branches off it, it tapered from about a one inch diameter to an eighth inch diameter and it sailed through the air like a lightweight spear. Of course one stroke of your wooden-stick sword would deflect it and cut it in half.

So the night raids went on, each side trying to sneak up on the other. When you got a shot with your spear, there wasn't much chance for a "kill" because the other person either blocked it with his shield or cut it in half with his sword. There was no real object to the game except that a dubious "victory" could be claimed when the other side had to call a truce to go get more spears.

And then on Saturday nights, when the older kids in the neighborhood came out bringing their younger brothers and sisters with them, we would play all those benign games like, green light red light, red rover red rover, jump and skip rope, Johnny-ride-the- pony (boys only), actors and actresses, kick the can, and all kinds of other fun stuff that we engaged in on each other's front porches or in the street.

Where it all started, Sicily. My Grandfather, Don Vincenzo (whom I was named after); my grandmother, Francesca; Uncle Al; Mom; and Mamie.

My mother and father at their wedding, 1917

Mom and Pop Speranza, eight children later

Young Vince at Public School 22, Staten Island, NY

3. GOING TO WORK

AT AGE 12, YOUR CHILDHOOD WAS OVER. DURING THE DEPRESSION, BY law, boys at age 12 were eligible for part-time working papers—twenty hours a week—a number no one paid attention to.

No different than all the other boys in the neighborhood, I went for mine. In those days at age 14, you could quit school after graduating from 8th grade and get a full-time job, providing you attended "continuation school" at night until age 16. Of course compulsory education laws now forbid all these working permits, but back then it was different, it was expected, and everybody did it willingly. Helping the family was priority number one.

Your mother took you up and down the neighborhood streets inquiring in all the stores if anyone needed the help of a "good, smart, strong, boy." Well, when my mother took me up and down the neighborhood streets, my first part-time job was at an importer-exporter grocery store. I had a bicycle that my brother put together from junkyard parts. Theoretically, I was to be a delivery boy. I worked every day after school from 3:00 to 6:00, all day Saturday from 7:00 in the morning to 11:00 at night, and half a day on Sunday from 9:00 to 1:00. My pay was $1.25 a week. Once I started to work, I became a different kid. I went to work right after school, got home at 6:30, ate my dinner by 7:00, did my homework until 9:00 and went to bed. My only "day off" was Sunday afternoon and that's when, for 25 cents, I took my brother and me to the movies, ten cents each, and a big bag of candy for a nickel.

Did it bother me? Did it hurt my childhood? Did I resent it? Absolutely not! When a little boy age 12 can come home and plunk a dollar and a quarter down on the table, I got to keep the quarter, and your father's only making eight dollars a week, you feel like you've been really helpful in getting the family through tough times. It makes you feel extra good.

I liked my job real well when delivering but, unfortunately, on

Sunday mornings, I had to mop floors, wash pots and pans, and clean the big refrigerators. In my house that was "women's work" and I never did it before. So I learned my first lessons about the real world. Lots of times you have to do certain things whether you want to or not.

I did learn some job skills that stood me in good stead later...like making sausage and mozzarella. My first job was an eye-opener.

Of course I had some misadventures along the way to age 12. My father, who managed to keep a job during the entire depression when 45% of Americans were out of work, unfortunately had to allow two and a half hours to get to work and two and a half hours to come home. He always had to get to work a half hour early to change clothes and have a smoke. It meant he left in the morning before any of us were up and he didn't get back home until seven or eight o'clock at night; just in time to eat a meal, smoke a cigarette and go to bed. We hardly saw him except for Sundays.

Pop always had a bottle of wine with his meal. My job was to fill that bottle of wine each day from the barrel in the cellar before he got home. Pop made his own wine and it was a whole- family affair. I had to go from upstairs and down three flights of stairs to the cellar. The cellar was dark and scary and had just one little light bulb in it. I was very little when I started doing this, probably no more than six or seven years old. I had received strict instructions, "You must never fill the bottle beyond the neck because you must leave space at the top for the wine to breathe, "Understand, Vinnie?"

"Yes, Pop."

So each day I would go down to the cellar, shiver a little bit at the darkness and spooks and creaky noises I heard, and do my job. I placed the funnel in the bottle, put the bottle in the right place under the spigot, turned it on, and watched very carefully until I got to the right spot on the bottle, turned it off, put the funnel back, put the cork in the bottle, and ran upstairs as fast as I could.

Well one day the inevitable happened, I didn't pay enough attention, and, the bottle filled all the way to the top! Oh God! Disaster! Panic!

What to do! I looked around to see if there was someplace I could pour it out, but that wasn't right. I just didn't know what else to do except

…the simple solution came fast. I tipped the bottle up to my mouth and drank it down to the proper level, put the cork in it, and ran upstairs.

When I got upstairs, my walking was a little erratic. Later my mother described it like this: *"Here comes this little kid with a bottle of wine in his hand and he is muttering, "Papa's going to kill me, Papa's going to kill me." When I said to him, "What For," he said nothing; he rolled his eyes and slid under the table and went to sleep. I ran to him wondering what was wrong, a little frightened. When I got close to him and smelled wine on his breath, I was relieved but angry and laughing all at the same time. I hollered at him, "At your age you started with the wine already," but he was fast asleep.*

I got "it" the next day.

Another time, I had my new sneakers on. Every summer when school was out, all the kids got a new $.29 pair of sneakers for the summertime. You had to be sure they lasted all summer because there was no more buying anything until school starts and you get a pair of shoes. I was out on my bicycle up at the gas station putting air in the tires, and they were tarring the road in front my house. I watched a little bit and when the tar truck went by I looked at that beautiful fresh tar and had a brilliant idea. I said to myself, "I'm going to step out there and very carefully get my sneakers in that nice tar and put a good coat of it on both the soles. They will last forever."

And so I did.

I ran home to show my mother. My mother saw me coming down the hall leaving a trail of tar and dirt. Just as I said, "Mom look, my sneakers are going to last forever," she let out a screech and wacked me. "Get out of this house." I was surprised, shocked, and hurt. Worse!

"Get a bucket with kerosene and a brush and sit out there and scrub all the tar off your sneakers, and then the hallway." I cried bitter tears at the injustice of the world. Oh what a bad day that was.

You must be made aware that during the Depression, if you fell or got into a fight, your primary concern when you went home was not, were you hurt, but did you rip any of your clothes. You learned to sew very early in life so as to try to get away with torn clothing before Momma got to see them.

One day my younger brother, Rocky, and I were fooling around on the porch. We both had on cotton broadcloth shirts that had seen their best days. They had endured many washings on the old scrub boards with octagon soap which is not very kind to cotton. In the roughhouse that followed, my brother grabbed the front of my shirt and it tore.

"Oh yeah…"

And I reached over and grabbed *his* shirt and tore it.

"Oh yeah…"

And he reached over and pulled the whole sleeve off *my* shirt.

In the ensuing few seconds, we tore each other's shirts to shreds, laughing and giggling all the way. Then, reality set in. How in the world were we going to explain to Mom what happened?

We knew what the result was going to be. How to avoid the inevitable? Very cleverly, we sent younger brother, Al, up to our room and told him to get each of us a sweater from our drawer. We buttoned on only the collar and cuffs of our now demolished shirts. Then we donned the sweaters, and permitted only the collar and cuffs to show. At the usual five o'clock dinner call we went upstairs and sat at the table. It was August and my mother began to look at us wearing sweaters. "What are you two doing with a sweater on?"

"Eh, it was a little chilly down on the porch."

Mama just shook her head and for a moment it looked like we were going to get away with it, until my stupid brother reaches for something on the table exposing the cuff of his shirt with no sleeve attached to it. The charade was over, and Momma was furious. We were dismissed from the table and "we got it."

So much for rough house wrestling.

And then there was my brother, Joey. He was seven years older and I worshiped him. I believe a good introduction to Joey would be to read the eulogy I delivered at his demise. (See "Eulogy to Joe" in appendix.)

An icon in all these childhood antics, in fact during all of our young lives was Momma's wooden spoon. It was about 18 inches long, made of some type of hardwood, probably oak. Ostensibly it was used to stir the pasta in the large spaghetti pots, but it had many other duties as well. It was the symbol of discipline and with it; Momma controlled the world we lived in.

When the family sat down to dinner, Pop sat at the head of the table, but Momma did not sit at the other end of the table, she sat at the middle of the table nearest to the kitchen. With her 18 inch spoon, she had a reach that encompassed everyone at any corner of the table. A quick light tap on the knuckles of the foolish child who tried to reach for something he should not have brought instant compliance. It didn't take long for all of us to learn good table manners at the sight of the spoon alongside Momma's plate. It was also her weapon of choice for any other breaches of the peace that took place in the house. Her mere mention of the spoon brought instant agreement to whatever she asked of her children. How else do you control eight children and have them grow up right?

I'll never forget one episode with momma's spoon. After the attic rooms had been fixed, my brother Joey, Rocky, and I had one room all to ourselves. We each had a single bed in the corners of the room. Now Pop's only day off was Sunday and we had strict orders about Sunday mornings. It was the only morning that Pop got to sleep a little later than usual. "Kids, don't get out of your rooms and <u>no noise</u> until after Pop gets up."

Awake early, we had to stay in our room until told that Pop was awake. Just picture three rambunctious boys trying to stay quiet for a couple of hours after waking up on a Sunday morning.

Inventions, inventions. My brother, Joey, wadded up some newspaper to about the size of a softball. He put rubber bands all around it until it made a good punch ball.

And then the rules; NO NOISE! Whoever had the ball was <u>up</u>, and he punched it as hard as he could toward one of the corners. He then had to jump to Joey's bed (first base), and then to Rocky's bed (second base), and then to Vinny's bed (third-base) *without touching the floor*. Whoever chased after the ball had to try to tag him along the way. Oh, what a fun game that was.

But without noise? Impossible. The game proceeded until, standing in the doorway, *Momma,* in that faded blue chenille robe, with her hands folded across her chest; in one of them, THE SPOON. "That's how you stay quiet to let Pop sleep?"

When she charged into the room with her weapon "at the ready" there was a mad scramble as each boy dived under his bed. Mamma was swinging away at the air, because we all disappeared. Her next move was to kneel at the bed and make broad sweeps under it to whack at us even though we were hugging the wall. She kept going from bed to bed, knowing she was not landing any blows but hearing with satisfaction our squeals and cries pretending we were being hit. This would continue briefly until she started laughing at the fun of it all. When all was quiet and she had made her point, she left, telling us to come on down to breakfast because this morning she was going to make pancakes (a rare treat, since most mornings during the Depression, breakfast consisted of cut up chunks of bread in a bowl of coffee).

P.S. Momma continued the use of her infamous spoon, even past the time that we boys were big enough to take it away from her, which I hasten to add, would be unthinkable. It was now symbolic, and we loved it. My father passed away first, my mother two years later. When the family gathered to share what our parents had left us, while everyone else asked for this and that, I had only one request, I wanted Momma's spoon. I got it and have it until this day.

A word about how we were really disciplined. Since Pop was not home most of the time, Momma was the disciplinarian. And Momma was a master at it. She knew just when and how much was needed to bring compliance and not resentment. Most of the time verbal admonishments were enough, but if not, there was always The Spoon.

But, the teeth in mama's discipline was one simple phrase, "You want me to tell Papa when he comes home?" That did it because Papa saw to it that at least on one occasion, each of the boys got to experience what it meant to disobey Momma. And it only had to happen once.

Mine came when I was about 10 or 11 years old. I was sitting on the empty overturned coal bucket reading a book. Momma, noticing the bucket I was sitting on was empty, asked me to go down to the basement and fill it up. I was warm and cozy near the stove, reading a good book, enjoying myself immensely, and hated the disturbance. Foolishly and recklessly, I said "no." Shocked, Momma said, "You want me to tell Papa when he gets home?"

"I don't care," I said, and went blithely on reading my book.

That evening when Papa came home, before he had even removed his coat, Momma told him. Without another word or gesture, Papa called me and asked me, did I say no to Momma. With Momma standing right there, I had to say *yes*. With one backhand I was sent sprawling to the floor under the table. I let out one yelp and started to cry. My sister started under the table with a cloth, but my father said, "Leave him alone." He faced the rest of the family and said, "Don't ever say no to Momma."

I never did ever again.

Cruel and unusual punishment? Absolutely not. The indelible impression made on me by that act influenced the rest of my childhood and then adulthood. When punishment is justified, swift and temporarily painful, you never forget it. Does it cause you to resent your parents? Of course not. No one loved their parents more than we did ours, and how many times after we grew up did we thank our parents again and again for the way in which we were raised. Of course when today's psychiatrists tell us that that was the wrong way, all I can do is compare what I see in the undisciplined children of today and the children of my day and shake my head.

To this day, every time I experience the smell of freshly baked bread, I shut my eyes, smile, and think of Grandma. Every Friday, Grandma baked the bread for the entire family; great big Sicilian loaves of bread with a hard crust that, if uncut, would keep the bread fresh for an entire week. Grandma had a special rule, that whichever of the kids got home first from school on Friday and helped her would get a special treat. I was the champion.

On Friday, I would push myself to the front of the class, and as soon as the bell rang, charge out of the school and run all the way home—about half a mile. None of my brothers and sisters ever beat me home. I would throw off my briefcase, take off my coat, and put on the apron that grandma had hanging on the door. Then I helped Grandma mash the yeast, knead the bread, tend to the fire so the oven was properly warmed, and anything else grandma asked me to do.

The treat? Grandma would take all the little scraps of dough left over, shape them into a small round loaf, and put it in the oven. When it was done, warm from the oven, she cut it open, spread olive oil on it, and then salt-and-pepper. And it was for me! Oh heavenly bliss. Nothing in this world before or after ever tasted so delicious.

Later in life, as an adult, I tried to duplicate that effort, but it never tasted the same. I have also tried my hand at baking bread with a good thick crust, but cannot even come close to Grandma's. How sad we all were when Grandma had a stroke and could no longer bake for the family. It took a lot of getting-used to, to eat store-bought bread.

4. THE TEENS

AFTER AGE 12, WHEN I ENTERED THE PART TIME SEMI-ADULT MODE; I went from grocery store delivery boy, to newspaper delivery boy, to soda jerk at the corner drugstore fountain, to usher at the Ritz Theater, and then to the National Guard as the war started—increasing my pay each time.

In elementary school, Public School 22, I did especially well. It was a neighborhood school, mostly Italian but with good representation from other groups. I received good grades, got along with all, and must have had some kind of dramatic talent because I was called upon to participate in all of the school plays, musicals, and other stage events. In the eighth grade I was elected mayor of the school in its experimental student government project. I appointed a city council, we wrote a constitution, and elected several sheriffs to uphold the law which was adjudicated by OUR Courts. What a wonderful experience for later life.

At Port Richmond High School however, it was another ballgame. When I entered it at age 14, I was working steadily after school and could not participate in any after school activities. It was pretty much a nose to the grindstone time with school, homework, and outside work. I didn't date as some of the other boys did; I must've been too shy. I believe part of it was also a little bit of prejudice from the high school girls. A lot of these girls were drawn from other neighborhoods like Norwegian, Swedish, Irish, and other non-Italian types. They were different from what I had been used to. They seemed to look down on us immigrant kids. I imagine I did not ask any of them for a date because I was afraid I would be turned down.

I think I was happy enough in my high school years, feeling important that I was still helping the family financially, getting reasonably good grades, and enjoying all kinds of family functions. I didn't need girlfriends.

Vince Speranza, teenage soda jerk, New York City, 1941

5. THE WAR

ON SUNDAY, DECEMBER 7, 1941, I WAS 16 YEARS OLD AND RIDING MY bicycle to Port Richmond to a Greek diner where I was to buy a dozen hotdogs with all the "fixings." My older brother and sister had chipped in the money to treat us young kids to these special hotdogs. When I walked into the restaurant, everybody was silent, listening intently, and paying no attention to me. The second time I asked the waiters for service, they said, "Shut up, we're listening to a special radio report. It sounds like the United States has been attacked by the Japanese."

I was shocked, forgot about the hotdogs, and bicycled home rapidly, shouting before I even got through the door, "Turn the radio on." My startled family gathered around the radio that I had just turned on, and listened intently to the various reports coming in. It sounded indeed like the United States had been attacked and the nation was waiting for our president to respond. Franklin D. Roosevelt did respond stating that "a state of war exists between the United States of America and the Empire of Japan."

What a bombshell! While in the past we had paid some attention to the war that began in 1939 in Europe, we really didn't think it was going to affect us. Now however, it was a different story.

When I went to school Monday morning, the usual noisy groups of kids were subdued. Some of our teachers were in tears. Our health education teacher, Mr. Bernstein, began teaching us close order drill instead of baseball. He told us that within a year most of us would be in the service. We thought the war would be over by then since once our B-17 bombers got to Japan, the war would be won. How naïve and uninformed we were.

In a few weeks, however, things began to return to normal. We listened to the war news on our radios, but were more concerned about our grades and graduation from high school. Some of us, like me, inquired about the National Guard, and how old you had to be to get in. We found that at age 17 you could join the National Guard. Eagerly we jumped at the chance and began to get a taste of military training while we were still in high school.

Boys started disappearing from our neighborhood as the draft claimed them as soon as they were 18. I just couldn't wait. I started hinting to my parents that I would like to quit school and volunteer for the Navy, which would take you at age 17, but they were opposed. Before my 18th birthday, I visited the draft board, and asked them if they could put my name at the top of the list for enlistment as soon as I turned 18. They said, oh yes, they could do that very easily.

Two weeks after my 18th birthday, March 23, 1943, I acted surprised and shocked that the letter from the War Department came which said, "Greetings; Uncle Sam needs you." I responded immediately that I was ready to go, but for some reason I was not inducted until October 1943. I found out later that because I had graduated from high school in January 1943 and did not turn 18 until March, my "student status" was extended to my entry into City College of New York. The Army would not take you in the middle of the semester and so I had to stay in school from January 1943 to June 1943, and wait until October for induction.

When the entire family was informed that I was to depart for the Service, oh what advice I was given.

Uncle #1, "Vin, take anything except the infantry."

Me, "Why if you want to get into the fight?"

Uncle # 1, "Because a lot of people get killed in the infantry."

Uncle # 2, "Try for the Navy, Vin."

Me, "I don't like the water, besides people get killed in the Navy, too."

Uncle # 2, "Yeah, but in between battles you always have a clean bed and good food."

Uncle # 3, "Try for the Air Force, Vin, if you're not a pilot you'll always be working at an airport which is usually plenty far back from the front lines."

Yeah, yeah, yeah…

During all this time my father said nothing. I started packing.

After the party everybody went home, giving me all kinds of blessings and religious support before they left. My father asked me what time we had to leave in the morning, and then told me to get a good night's sleep.

Sleep? Impossible. I was about to enter a new and strange life and had no idea what it really held.

The next morning, everybody was up before me; the girls were crying, my brothers were trying not to, and my mother was all red-faced but trying to smile. My father told everybody to say goodbye to me at the house because only <u>he</u> was to accompany me to the train station. I kissed all my sisters and my mother, shook hands and hugged all my brothers, and went out the door with my father.

All the way to the train station, he said not one word. When the train came and I got aboard, he still hadn't said anything, but as the train started to leave, he leaned over and said to me in Italian, "Non fai mai una cosa que mi fa calari la testa." (Just Don't Do Anything To Make Me Hang My Head In Shame).

I lost it as I tried to say, "I won't, Pop."

And then for the first time in my life I saw tears in my father's eyes as he disappeared from view down the train station. You don't know how many times I relived that scene during the war.

I tried hard and sincerely hope that I never did anything to make him ashamed of me.

When I arrived at City Hall in lower Manhattan, they herded us into a large room and administered the oath. We solemnly promised to protect and defend the Constitution of the United States. I WAS IN!

After a whole batch of paperwork, they put us on buses and shipped us to Camp Shanks, New York. In a flurry of activity we were given shots, uniforms, and a battery of tests. The next day an officer sat down with me and went over my test results.

"Speranza, do you know that you did 97.1 on the mechanical aptitude test? You like tanks?"

Me, "Yes, Sir."

The officer, "Do you know you did 96.9 in the radio aptitude test. You like the Signal Corps?"

Me, "Yes, Sir."

The officer, "You also did well in math and science; you like the Artillery?

Me, "Yes, Sir."

Then he took a big stamp and marked my papers "INFANTRY" (which was what I wanted anyway). So much for choice.

After a few more days of sorting out, learning serial numbers, and trying to get to know one another; the word came down. "Check the bulletin board for your name and where you are to report tomorrow morning at 0600 for assignment." I was to board a train for the Infantry School at Fort Benning, Georgia. For the first time in my life I was going to be more than a few miles from New York City and I was really excited about it.

Now it began.

6. THE ARMY

TO THIS DAY I STILL MARVEL AT HOW IN THE WORLD THE ARMY DID SO well at turning raw civilians into soldiers. How they accomplished the fantastic task of moving thousands of men, providing them with food, clothing, and shelter, and then getting them to where the fighting is, must be admired by all. The logistics were staggering.

When we arrived at Fort Benning, a group of sergeants was waiting for us, and quickly maneuvered us to a compound. Your last name was called out, you responded with your first name, middle initial, and your serial number.

"Speranza?"

"Vincent J 42049550."

"Barracks Number 14, Training Company C, Third platoon, Second squad. Move out!"

"Yes, sir."

And then, at last, Infantry training.

We were issued a rifle, the Garand M1, but were told that our first experience on the firing range would be with an old Springfield 1903.

There is the right way, the wrong way, and the Army way—and don't you ever argue with that!

Calisthenics, close order drill, and learning to march with the full field packs and equipment. I loved it all. I never forgot the speech that our First Sergeant gave us before the training started. "You guys got 19 weeks with me, and I've got to turn you raw shits into soldiers. Remember this; if anybody is going to stick the limber dick to anybody it's going to be Mastorelli that does all the sticking. You got it?"

And we learned that Mastorelli meant it. Nobody got away with anything. Clean uniforms, clean rifles, stand at attention, and do what you're told. Then the serious part of the training began. How to kill a man with a rifle, with a bayonet, with the hand grenade, or with your bare hands. All the while, training films kept showing us the toughness of the German and Japanese armies and the dangers of venereal disease. Thirty mile night hikes with full field pack and rifles. Nine mile day runs. We started to really toughen up.

I made some friends, like Arcaro from Philly, and Tate from Ohio, and Thorpe from Florida. We didn't know it at the time but we were in a specialized unit called the Army Specialized Training Program. We weren't sure what it meant, but we were flattered that it seemed to be a special unit. Of course we sang, "Oh take down your service flag mother, your son's in the ASTP."

It didn't last long. At the end of the 19 weeks we were shipped to a regular line infantry outfit, the 87th Infantry Division at Fort Jackson, South Carolina—the "Acorn Division."

Oh that first furlough home. The family went crazy. Everybody thumping me on the back and telling me how good I looked in my uniform with the crossed rifles of the infantry on my lapel. My mother kept asking me about what I was eating. My brothers kept asking me about weapons. My sisters wanted to know how many girls I had been out with, and *my father said nothing*. He later told me he was very worried that since Italy had entered the war on the side of Germany I might be sent to Italy and end up killing some of his relatives. My response was simple, "They're the enemy, Pop. We're Americans." He shrugged his shoulders and walked off. It didn't happen; I did not fight in Italy.

And now the waiting. Advanced training, advanced weapons training, advanced psychological warfare training, advanced gas and gas mask training. No hint as to when we were going overseas. We were becoming very impatient.

One day instead of taking us to the regular training grounds, we were marched out to a big field and told to sit down, there was going to be a demonstration. "What kind of demonstration?" we asked.

"Shut up and sit down."

After about half an hour, three C47 transports came roaring out of the western sky. When they were over our field, our jaws dropped in amazement as the plane doors opened and men spilled out in parachutes. They landed, rolled, discarded their chutes, and doubled-timed over to us to stand at attention. We were flabbergasted.

Paratroopers were new to the Army then, and here they were in front of us; magnificent men in sharp uniforms, brilliantly shined boots, and glittering silver wings on their chests.

Their lieutenant said, "We're looking for a few good men who have had advanced infantry training and want to join an all-volunteer parachute unit. All of us looked at each other, all of us thinking the same thing: Throw yourself out of an airplane hoping a piece of silk will land you safely? Why not! Can you think of a quicker way to get into the fight?

With some hesitation some hands started up, mine among them, but not all the way up yet. The lieutenant then said, "And there's an extra fifty dollars a month jump pay." All the hesitant hands went up the rest of the way immediately. We had joined the parachute troops!

The next morning we were sent by train back to Fort Benning, Georgia, except this time to a section set aside for parachute training. Fear of the unknown? Yeah, but excited about being in a real fighting outfit. Question about whether you could make it or not? Sure, they said the training is really tough, and guys "washed out" every day, but hell, how much worse could it be than advanced infantry training. The only question was, when the time comes, will you jump out of the airplane?

It was a five weeks course. First week was all physical training. In the Infantry you *walk* everywhere, in the Paratroops you *run* everywhere. In the Infantry you do 30 mile hikes; the Paratroops you do 50 mile hikes. Every morning before breakfast, strip to the waist and run nine miles to the town and back. Every infraction, even rolling your eyeballs at the sergeant, you do 50 push-ups.

"Speranza, what state are you from?"

"New York, sir."

"What a lousy state. Give me 50 push-ups for being from New York."

You get on the ground and do fifty push-ups; the sergeant does them with you. When you get up he asks, "Did you cheat?"

"No, sir."

"You jackass, gimme fifty push-ups for not cheating when you had a chance."

Of course, if you had said you *did* cheat, then fifty push-ups for cheating.

The second week was more physical training and on-the-ground jump training. There was an aircraft fuselage on the ground and we learned to go out the door, half turn to the left, and roll when you hit the ground.

The third week was jumping off a six-foot wall and rolling. Getting into a harness and jumping off a tower with a long cable along which you bounced until you hit the ground. And then the actual parachute towers where you got into a parachute harness and were released in an open chute to the ground.

The fourth week was parachute packing. When they told us that we would be packing the parachute that we were going to make our first jump in, you never saw a more attentive class in your whole life.

The fifth week was Showtime.

The Friday night before, you very carefully packed your parachute, put your name on it, and then had the whole weekend to worry about it until Monday morning. Monday morning was *THE DAY*. Your first jump!

You reported to the C47 that was warming up on the tarmac. You strapped on your parachute and your reserve chute. You checked it and checked it and rechecked it.

You lined up and climbed clumsily on board. 18 men to the "stick"— two sticks in each plane. The plane took off and the sergeant said, "The smoking lamp is lit." I don't smoke, but I saw everybody else put a cigarette in his mouth and relax. "Hey, gimme a cigarette. I want to smoke, too." I lit up a cigarette, coughed, choked and got dizzy. The sergeant hollered, "The smoking lamp is out."

"First stick, stand up, hook up, check equipment." *No time to think about anything now, the moment had come.*

The last man in the stick checked the equipment of the man in front of him, tapped him on the shoulder, and said, "18 okay." Then each man in front of him said the same thing, "17 okay, 16 okay, 15 okay, etc." When it got down to number one, the jump master said, "Number One, Stand in the Door!" (I was number three). There were two lights at the door, a red one and the green one. The red one was lit, but when the green one came on, it was time to go. The jump master sat back with his foot raised, letting you know that if there was any hesitation, his foot would send you right out the door.

Greenlight. "Go, Go, Go!" My turn came, I moved right up to the door, made a half turn to the left, ducked my head so the tail of the plane wouldn't slice it off, and jumped. I counted, "1000, 2000, 3000," put my hand on the handle of the reserve chute which I would pull if the main didn't open, but the static line broke off, the prop blast opened the parachute, and I swung under it with just a slight jerk. *What a magnificent moment!*

You looked up; you saw all that beautiful white silk against a pale blue sky, absolute stillness and quiet, and you floated gently and gracefully toward the ground. You smiled and smiled and smiled. This was what all the training was about and you had come through with flying colors. What a feeling!

Suddenly everything was interrupted by the ground coming up at you pretty fast. More training kicks in. You grabbed the risers of your chute and prepared to land as they had taught you. Keep your legs and feet together, bend your knees slightly. When you hit the ground continue to bend your knees, tuck in your elbows, and roll over. Get up and spill the air out of your chute from the bottom. Release the harness. Roll up your parachute and double time off the field. You had made your first jump and you had neither shit your pants nor pissed on your boots, for which you are eternally grateful!

Talk about an exciting afternoon. And to think that tomorrow morning you're going to be able to do it all over again. You shout and laugh out loud, "I'm a paratrooper!" But then, with caution, "Of course I've got three more day jumps to go and one night jump, so let's not celebrate yet."

The next day was marvelous. Confidence that you had already passed the first test, less tension, don't need to choke on a cigarette, and anticipation of that beautiful sight of blue sky and a large canopy of sturdy silk with parachute cords, made you smile.

And, *I packed it myself!*

The officer, "Speranza."

Me (gratefully; some got "washed out" on the first jump), "Vincent J 42049550."

The officer, "Get aboard."

"Smoking lamp's lit, the smoking lamp's out, standup, hook up, stand in the door." Once again, that half turn to the left, the head ducked down, "1000, 2000, 3000," the static line breaks away, the prop blast fills the chute, and once again that beautiful scenario of blue sky and stillness as you swing under the parachute. This time you pay attention to smoke that was generated on the ground to give you the wind direction. This time you try to guide your chute by pulling on the risers a little bit so as to land closer to the trucks. This time the ground comes up a little faster than you remember and before you know it you're on the ground, you roll, you gather up your chute, and double time off the field, grinning from ear to ear. Oh what a glorious thing to be a paratrooper.

The third and fourth days were repeat performances and now you felt like an old hand. One more jump Friday night, and Saturday morning you would receive your wings and the exclusive right to blouse your pants on those new jump boots.

Friday night! A little less cocky tonight. There was a bright moon but you were a little less sure of yourself. What was it going to be like to come down in the dark? What about all those warnings of mistaking trees for bushes, and not crossing your legs and hiding your face, resulting in getting pretty banged up landing in a tree. And how about if you landed in the Chattahoochee River which is near the drop zone; would you remember to release your harness, hold onto your risers, and let go of the chute when you were six feet above the water so that the wind would blow it away and not tangle you up and drown you?

Well, you took the cigarette this time, puffed on it as though you knew how to inhale but didn't, and stamped it out angrily when the smoking lamp went out. This time you made the sign of the cross as you moved up to the door.

Out, jolt, jerked upright a little bit, but still swinging under the chute as the prop blast filled it. Look for the lights on the ground. Steer toward them. Not too close now, you don't want to land on one of the trucks. You can now make out that you're going to land in a field, no tall bushes or trees in sight, but damn that ground is coming up fast. They told you that when you jump at night the air is "thinner" and you come down faster; I guess they're right.

No more time to think, bend the knees, hold onto the risers, bang, roll, spill the air out of the chute, roll it up and double time off the field. *Goddammit you made it!*

This time the smile split your face wide open. You're going to graduate tomorrow morning. You're a full-fledged god-damned *paratrooper*. Won't the guys in the neighborhood shit in their pants when they see you <u>this</u> time. Oh man, oh man, oh man. As the song says, "I am happy as a lark believe-eve me, as we go rolling, rolling home."

Too excited to sleep much that night and a little sad when we heard that two of our guys, in the moonlight, mistook a concrete highway for the Chattahoochee River, let go of their chutes too soon, and splattered themselves on the road. Terrible tragedy, but nothing could really dampen what was going to happen Saturday morning.

(The officer): "Speranza."

(Me): "Vincent J 42049550"

"Congratulations, Trooper, you are Airborne now, don't ever forget it"

I want to tell you, I was 10 feet tall and weighed 300 pounds, with muscles of iron and steel, and ready to take on the whole god-damned Nazi army all by myself!

We were given weekend passes and you never saw a prouder bunch of guys walking around that town of Columbus, Georgia. In the following week we were told that there would be one more seven-day furlough home, one more advanced parachute jump, and then overseas. No news could've made us happier. You cannot believe how anxious we were to go home and show off our new uniforms, paratrooper boots, and silver wings. However, a couple of days home and we found ourselves longing to get back to the outfit. There was a job to do and we were now equipped to do it. *Let's go, we don't want to be left out.*

When we got back we made one more jump with full field equipment, backpacks, rifles, and helmets. No sweat! The next thing we knew, we were on a train heading for somewhere on the East Coast to find a boat. We ended up at Camp Upton, not an hour and 45 min. from my house in New York City. And now the waiting begins again.

My friends started to recall that, while we were at Fort Benning, every time the meal was spaghetti, I would snort and say it was a sorry excuse for the real thing. "If we ever get near New York City, I will take you home and give you a taste of real spaghetti." So it began. "All right, Speranza, what about all that bullshit you used to give us that if we got anywhere near New York City you would let us taste some real spaghetti?"

"All right, all right, let me call my mother."

I got on the phone, "Hello, Mom. I'm stationed only about two hours away and might be able to get a pass to come home for just one day."

"Oh how wonderful, Vinnie, are you coming today?"

"Yes."

"Say Mom, I've been telling the guys that if we were ever in New York that I would bring them home to taste some of your real spaghetti. Can I bring some of the guys with me?"

"Sure, how many?"

"About eighteen." (That's how many guys were in my "stick" when we jumped)

"Eighteen?? How much time do I have?"

"Oh it will take us at least three or four hours before we get there."

"Three hours? Plenty of time. Bring them all."

And so, three hours later, eighteen young paratroopers show up at my mother's modest house. All my sisters went bananas, and my brothers stood in awe. You can't believe how Mom accommodated all eighteen of us. She had tables coming out of the kitchen to the dining room and into the living room. She had planks between two chairs which would seat five at a time. And she and my sisters had the most magnificent spaghetti dinner on the table as soon as we got there. How proud I was. The boys couldn't sing the praises loud enough and my mother gloried in it all.

When dinner was over, we put on a demonstration of a jump. We lined up at the dining room entrance and "stood in the door," chanted "1000, 2000, 3000," half turn to the left and out the door. My family loved it.

Then my mother's penetrating look held the eyes of every one of those boys.

"When was the last time you wrote your mother a letter?"

Everyone stammered. "Don't anybody move," said Mom as she ran upstairs and came down with paper and envelopes and a bunch of pens and pencils and said, "Every one of you *right now*, write your mother a letter…and you too," she said to me. Dutifully, we all complied. She did not trust us to mail them, so she gathered them all and said she would mail them herself. It was one of our last evenings in the United States and the memory of it stood us in good stead in the days ahead.

7. OVERSEAS

BY NOW IT WAS OCTOBER 1944. ONE MORNING THEY LOADED US ONTO A train for the NYC docks where the Queen Mary, now a converted troopship, was waiting for us. We caught a glimpse of the Statue of Liberty as we left New York Harbor. All of us were very quiet, wondering the same thing; would we ever see her again? Reality was setting in.

The seven days I spent on the Queen Mary were memorable only because they were pretty boring. We did nothing but stand in line almost all day. In the morning, by 6:00 AM, you got in line with your mess gear for breakfast. The line went from A deck almost the length of the ship to B deck to C deck, or at least it seemed that way, before you got to the kitchen. It took almost two hours and then you received some powdered eggs, two link sausages stuffed with 50% breadcrumbs, and a cup of tea. By 9:30 you were out of there and in line again to wash your mess gear. That took another two hours before you got to the three barrels of treated water where you washed your gear and then tried to find your way back to your cabin.

The cabin, by the way, was one of the original two-person 12' x 12' staterooms that now had 15 pipe-rack bunks, five on each wall, minus the wall that had the doorway and bathroom. Thirty men were assigned to each state room with all of their gear, including rifles, duffel bags, and helmets. Fifteen men slept in the bunks while the other fifteen slept on deck. The next night you reversed the procedure. You can imagine the chaos in those rooms - fifteen guys, gear of thirty men, and a crap game going on in the middle of the floor.

By two o'clock you got in line again. A deck, B deck, C deck...and so on and so on for seven days. There was a PX on board that sold soda, candy, and cookies, but the lines were so long we never bothered to even try. We let the two meals a day take care of our needs.

There was only one bright spot; Mickey Rooney was aboard as a regular GI. He and his group put on a show for us. I met him in the chow line one day; a real nice guy.

We were warned about standing too close to the rail, because if you fell overboard, the Queen stopped for no one. They would throw down a life raft and wish you bon voyage. On deck, many guys spent their time carving their initials on the wooden handrail that surrounded the ship. I understand that after the war, this handrail was removed and put in a museum somewhere in London. My name is not on it.

Finally we docked off the coast of Scotland, were taken ashore by two smaller craft, and put on a train to "somewhere in England." We later found out it was the small town of Hungerford.

It was November 1944. The Quonset huts we were in were cold and dreary. We were allowed passes to the nearby towns of Reading and Brighton. We waited and waited to be sent to France to join the 101st Airborne Division, now fighting in Holland. Each day they would line us up and the sergeant would say, "All right, every man willing to volunteer for a dangerous mission, take one step forward." We would all step forward. And the sergeant would say, "All right, that's good, we'll let you know." But nothing ever happened. We found out later, that they were contemplating jumping us into Holland to support the losing battle taking place in the failed Market Garden campaign. It was not to be.

What else happened in Hungerford during those weeks we were waiting to get into the fight? One night, coming home from an all-night pass about half drunk, we arrived at the camp just before reveille. The latrine at that time was a long building with a platform with holes in it about three feet apart which served as the toilet. Each hole had a "honey bucket" under it which was replaceable from the outside. Early every morning an old Englishman with a flat-bed wagon and a horse would gather up the filled "honey buckets," load them on the wagon, and place new ones under each hole.

Well, this morning as he sleepily went by, the horse had a big erection almost touching the ground. One of our guys thought it would be funny to whack that poor horse's erection with a stick. Oh how we laughed when the horse reared up and went galloping down the road throwing honey buckets of crap in all directions with the old Englishman hollering "whoa, whoa, whoa!" What a dirty trick that was; we should have all been court-martialed.

The only real memorable incident at Hungerford was when two of my buddies and I had a weekend pass to Brighton. Brighton was a seaside town, buttoned up at night because of the blackout, but, we were told, was "lively." So the three of us went to a pub and ordered a "bitters" which was the warm beer that everyone else was drinking. We noticed that there was a fireplace with a bunch of iron pokers in it which the Englishmen from time to time would draw out, place in their beer, and then put back in the fire. What the hell are they doing, we thought, the beer is hot enough as it is.

We later found out it was a tradition. So, when in Rome do as the Romans, and we stuck hot pokers in our beer; all the while looking around for the ladies. As healthy young males, we were searching for female companionship. When none appeared, we finally asked one of the old Englishman where the ladies were. "The ladies don't come in here, this is a pub. If you want the ladies, you must go down the road to the dance hall."

"Oh," we said. "Thank you."

Down at the dance hall, it was another ballgame—music, dancing, and lots of ladies. The way in which it ended however was three of us and only two ladies. I very magnanimously said, "Go ahead boys, you take off; I'll go back to the pub and have another drink." (As a matter of fact, I was still a virgin at that time, and wasn't sure about how to make out with the ladies anyway).

Back at the pub I proceeded to get gloriously drunk. I found a couple of guys who liked to sing, as I did, and we had a ball singing *It's A Long Way to Tipperary, Pack Up Your Troubles in Your Old Kit Bag, There'll always be an England,* and the U.S. Army caisson song. About four o'clock in the morning I staggered out of the place and got jumped by three or four guys who proceeded to beat me up. Then they took my watch, my money, and my pass which was in the wallet. They left me lying in the alley next to the pub.

It was daylight when I staggered to my feet, wiped the blood off the side of my head, and wandered down the hill as the path of least resistance. At the bottom of the hill was a little park called Queens Terrace, a pond, and a stone bench facing the road. I sat down on the bench wondering what I was going to do when the MP patrols started their rounds. Without my pass I was AWOL.

At about that time an old Englishman came by walking his dog. "I say, Yank, are you all right?" he said.

"No! I responded, considering some of your young toughs just beat the hell out of me, took my money, my pass, and my wallet, and I'm now AWOL."

He was horrified. "Oh, Yank, that's terrible," he said. "I am so sorry. Please come home with me; I only live up the street a ways, you can wash up and my wife will clean and press your uniform." Anxious to get off the street before the MP patrols came, I accepted.

His name was Radbourne and he had a wife and three children. He had been badly wounded while with the British Army in Africa and was now discharged. His wife did indeed clean and press my uniform, wash the blood off the side of my head, and then they put out a meal that I couldn't believe. This was at a time when the British were being rationed to one egg per week and a quarter pound of tea per month. They must've used a whole month's ration to put that dinner on the table, Yorkshire pudding and all.

I never forgot it. That evening he took me in his car to where the trucks were waiting to take us back to camp. I got back to camp without getting into trouble. Thank you, Mr. Radbourne.

The following week, I revisited the Radbournes, bringing with me a box of whatever groceries our mess sergeant would give me, including a five pound package of tea. The Radbournes and I thanked each other again and again, took each other's addresses, and promised to stay in touch. We exchanged some pictures. No further contact until 65 years later. More about that in another chapter.

The days wore on but finally, in the last week of November, we were flown to France to join the Division as it was coming out of Holland. I was assigned to H Company, 501st Parachute Infantry Regiment, 101st Airborne Division. I was proud!

8. BATTLE AT LAST

THE 101ST AIRBORNE DIVISION WAS IN BAD SHAPE. IT HAD LOST A LOT OF men and equipment. It had been in combat for 72 days in Holland. Although it had successfully taken and held its assigned objectives, the bridges into Germany, the Market Garden Operation had failed. The Germans had cut off the road that British armor was to use coming up to relieve the lightly armed parachute divisions. Giving up those bridges rankled in their throats as they thought about how many men they had lost for nothing. They were in no mood to welcome the replacements like me who were to take the place of the buddies they had just lost.

I didn't feel too bad. I had been forewarned. Until you prove yourself in combat, a veteran organization does not pay much attention to you.

We were at camp Mourmelon in France, a former German barracks during the occupation. While licking its wounds, the Division was to get some R&R. Some passes were issued to visit newly liberated Paris, and Rheims, or to the dreary little town of Mourmelon. The Division began to plan recreational activities like baseball, football, and races. Equipment was turned in for repair and replacements were to be integrated into their units and given combat training. A highlight event, which was announced in a brochure (I still have a copy), was that the entire show of the Follies Bergere was to be brought to camp Mourmelon for the entertainment of the troops. It never happened.

Barely three weeks out of Holland, the Division, under strength, ill-equipped, no winter clothing, short supplies of food and ammo, with many of its weapons turned in for repair, was alerted again!

It was four o'clock in the morning, still pitch black outside, and the barracks lights went on. "All right, drop your cocks and grab your socks. We're moving out!" shouted the First Sergeant.

Groans and moans from all over the barracks, "You're crazy, the ground is frozen, we'll all break our legs."

41

"We're not jumping, we're going up in trucks."

"But, Sarge, I got no rifle."

"I got no machine gun."

"I got no overcoats or galoshes, or a helmet," came from all over the barracks.

"Stop bitching; make a list of what you need and we'll stop along the way to pick it up."

"Fallout in 30 minutes with whatever gear you have and lineup by platoons."

We threw on whatever clothing we had, picked up whatever gear we had, bitched and bitched and bitched under our breaths, and moved out into the cold. There was a line of big trucks out there, motors running, and sergeants and officers all over the place keeping us moving. These were open trucks, no cover, and they packed us in there like sardines. Some of us chose to stand up, leaning over the edge of the truck, while others sat and still others lay down. Those of us standing were later to regret our decision.

The line of trucks finally started moving and we shivered in the morning cold. I had a sweater and a field jacket, a pair of cotton pants, combat boots, no gloves, no beanie (wool cap for under the helmet), and that damn ice cold helmet on my head. Worse, I was a machine gunner with no machine gun!

We rode and rode, no stops, as we had suspected, not even a piss-call. Those of us who could hold it no longer, peed in our helmets and then attempted to throw it overboard with disastrous results. Tempers flared as more and more of us attempted to sit or lie down on the crowded floor of the truck. We were amazed that all the trucks had their lights on. We knew we were moving toward a combat zone. If the Luftwaffe was around, we would be literally sitting ducks.

And then there was the scuttlebutt. No one knew where we were going, why we were going, and why we were being sent somewhere understrength and underequipped. All kinds of wild theories flew about. Eisenhower had been captured and we had to rescue him. We were being moved up to be the first ones into Berlin. The Germans had surrendered and we were to escort all the prisoners back to France.

But why us? Surely there were other outfits more combat-ready than we were at that particular time.

No one could have guessed that the Germans had broken through the Ardennes and were on their way to Antwerp which, if successful, would have divided the British armies in the north from the American armies in the South and given the Germans all the food, gasoline and equipment they needed from our stores at Antwerp, probably prolonging the war for another two to three years. The Battle of the Bulge had begun.

Finally a stop. We jumped off the truck and relieved ourselves all over the place. Some of the sergeants poured gasoline on the ground and lit it; we warmed our hands. Questions about when we would pick up the equipment and clothing we needed went unanswered. Back on the trucks. On and on. Just before daylight the trucks stopped. How happy we were to get off those cramped, cold miserable open trucks and move about.

"All right, both sides of the road, five yards apart, and watch out for snipers."

"But lieutenant, I haven't got a machine gun."

"Stop bitching and get in line, we'll get one off a disabled tank as soon as we can."

As it's getting light we walk into this little town with a sign that says "Bastogne."

"Where the hell is Bastogne?"

"Beats the shit out of me."

As we entered the town, an amazing sight confronted us. Hundreds of American troops and vehicles were all going the other way.

"Hey," we hollered, "the war is up this way." They all look dazed and demoralized. We began to realize that these were the men the Germans had just smashed through and beaten to a pulp. We felt sorry for them, and then, a bright idea. They were going back so they didn't need the weapons and ammunition some of them were still carrying.

We boldly stepped up to them took their rifles off their shoulders and their bandoleers of ammunition and said, "You won't need these and we do." We took their grenades and even some helmets. We patted them on the back and thanked them for their contribution. I "borrowed" a machine gun, and a lot of boys who had been unarmed now had weapons and ammunition.

Daylight brought more cold and snow flurries. My regiment, the 501st was the first sent out of town to "develop the situation" as our Colonel Ewell was ordered to do by General McAuliffe. The Germans were one day away, we had gotten there just-in-time to set up a defensive position before they hit us.

"H" Company was set up near Mont on a ridge and told to dig in. What a job digging a foxhole in frozen ground. It was three o'clock in the morning before we finished and set up the machine gun. Unbelievably, we got the word to, "Pack up we're changing position." Groans and moans, swearing under your breath, and doing as you're told.

"Okay, dig in here now." Another two hours digging another foxhole. We were cold, hungry, and exhausted when, unbelievably, we get the word to move to another position. Totally exhausted, we just scraped the snow aside and lay down. The hell with it.

It was now December 19, 1944, and the Germans had arrived. It had snowed all night and everything was covered. Where we finally dug our last foxhole, the ground sloped downward about 400 yards and then sloped upward toward the opposite ridge where the Germans were expected. We set our machine gun sights for 400 yards and waited.

I don't know what I felt. Nervous, scared, tough, hot, cold, confident, inadequate, and then my father's solemn face saying, *"Just don't do anything to make me hang my head in shame."*

"I won't, Pop."

The fog and mist began to lift in the early morning and then we heard the most dreaded sound that any infantryman can hear—the clank and squeal of the bogie wheels on tanks. We couldn't see them yet but the sound carried across the open field. And then the even worse sound of the big 88 mm artillery pieces being fired, and then a few seconds later a terrible explosion near you. Their artillery began a bombardment to supplement the tanks. The ground shook with explosions. All we could do was crouch down in our foxholes as low as we could and pray we didn't get a direct hit. When the bombardment ceased, we knew the German troops were now on their way. I chambered a round into my machine gun and waited for the lieutenant to give the word because German infantry was now crossing the field.

"Not yet," said the lieutenant.

The Germans were approaching the 400 yard mark. What they didn't know and we didn't know either, was that where the ground started sloping up toward us, there was a series of barbed wire fences buried by the snow.

When the first wave of the German troops hit those fences, it stopped them. We watched them struggling to get themselves off the wire when the second wave came up. They were attempting to help their buddies get off the fence. I was dying to pull the trigger but the lieutenant kept saying, "Not yet. Not yet."

When the third wave of German troops came up to the fence, you now had knots of men tangled in snow and barbed wire. "Now!" shouted the lieutenant.

Everything we had opened up on those Germans. It was a slaughter. The snow turned red. We kept pouring it on. I now noticed myself, exhilarated, snarling, smiling, cursing, cursing and firing, and traversing the field to get as many of them as possible. I didn't even seem to notice that German tank fire and artillery were still pounding us, causing all kinds of casualties. Tree bursts were raining down all around us. How in hell I was still not hit with something was a miracle! Medics were running all over the place. I even saw a priest giving a soldier last rites right out there in the open field.

Our artillery opened up and we continued to pour it on.

The German attack faltered, stopped, and then retreated. Bodies were lying all over the place, German and American.

They never tried a frontal attack like that again.

However, the real battle was just starting.

The snow came down steadily, the temperature continued to drop and the Germans made probing attacks day and night on all sides of the perimeter. When we saw that our wounded were not being evacuated, we finally understood that we had been surrounded. Surrounded by seven German divisions, three of them Panzers.

Reactions? "Yeah they got us surrounded, the poor bastards," one trooper was supposed to have said.

"We're supposed to be surrounded, we're paratroopers," said another.

As for myself? "Bring it on you bastards. Up to now you had it all your own way coming from Germany with 25 divisions, smashing through inexperienced or otherwise worn-out American troops that were in that sector. But now you're up against the 101st Airborne Division and that's another ballgame; got it Kraut?" Can you believe it; after just one battle I saw myself as a tough, cocky, real paratrooper veteran, worthy of the wings I wore.

Evidently the German strategy now was to bomb and shell the hell out of us from all sides and smash our resistance. They seemed to have plenty of ammunition. While their probing attacks continued looking for a weak spot in our lines, their artillery, mortars, and aerial bombardment leveled the town.

What General McAuliffe did was draw a small number of men from each unit to create a mobile reserve force backed with our limited number of tanks and tank destroyers. They rushed to the aid of any spot on the line that was seriously threatened.

The lines held, but ammunition was running low, and so was food.

An even worse threat was the weather. It stayed below zero most of the time. We were later told that it had been the coldest winter in Europe in twenty years. Almost no one had a winter coat. Most of us had only a field jacket, a sweater, and cotton longjohns. We had no gloves, no wool beanies, and no galoshes. Our feet were always wet, and we lost almost as many men to trench foot as to bullets. I was lucky in one respect because, just before we left the barracks, I picked up a pair of spare wool socks that I had hanging next to my bed. Those extra socks saved me from being a casualty, I'm sure. Each night I would take off my wet socks and put them inside my shirt against my belly and put on the dry ones. By the next night, those wet ones would be dry and I was able to change again. It made a difference.

There is another aspect to the miseries of that battle that most people don't realize.

The ubiquitous K-ration was a marvel of battlefield rations. It consisted of three units: a breakfast unit, a lunch unit, and a dinner unit. Inside of a waterproof waxed cardboard box, difficult to open, especially with frozen fingers, were three cigarettes, matches, a packet of powdered coffee, two small pieces of hard candy, three "dog biscuits," and—the biggest joke of all—a small piece of brown paper, no bigger than your hand nor thicker than a tea napkin, which was supposed to serve as toilet paper.

There was also a small round tin about the size of a tuna fish can that, in the breakfast unit, contained chopped ham and eggs, very greasy when cold. The lunch unit consisted of the same but a can of cheese, and the dinner unit had a can of pork loaf, also very greasy. If they could be heated, they weren't bad, but there was no way to do that. So, the breakfast unit gave you the runs, the dinner unit cheese would bind you up, and the supper unit would loosen you up again.

Not too bad. But the problem was you would never get three units in the proper sequence. After the third day we did not get more than two units a day. You can't imagine what it was like. In addition to everything else that you had to put up with, every couple of hours or so, you had to drop your pants and go. The man who had an extra cheese unit had gold, and he demanded a high price for it, usually in terms of cigarettes. In addition to the inconvenience, there was always the threat of "incoming" and the dive for your foxhole with your pants down.

The Luftwaffe did its share to add to the problems with random night bombing. It didn't seem to have specific targets; the town was already leveled, but just keeping us awake and harassed. We never did get any sleep really; it was just moments of dozing here and there. Even water was a problem. It would freeze in your canteen and you had to put it between your legs to warm it up a little in order to drink. Lots of times a handful of snow would have to suffice.

One night while moving our squad to another position, we all had an "unlucky" day with the K rations and had to "go" badly. We kept yelling at the sergeant, "Sergeant, we gotta go!"

"Not here," he would yell back.

Finally, in the moonlight, we saw a small field that had a haystack in it. We could wait no longer. "Sarge, we have to go right now!" And all of us proceeded to drop our pants to let nature take its course.

At that moment a brilliant flare went up from the German side and lit up the entire field. "Hit the dirt!" someone yelled, and everyone fell forward. The mortar shells began to land. As one of the last to go down, I will never forget the image of all those glistening white asses in the snow and everybody complaining of his balls being frozen. We got over it. Nobody had gotten hurt and we had another thing to talk about.

I think it was the third day that my friend, Joe Willis, was hit. On one of my trips to the headquarters, I went to look for him. I found him on the floor of the church, wrapped in one blanket and what looked like a curtain from one of the houses.

"Hey Joe, how are you doing?"

"Aw it's nothing, just a couple of small pieces of shrapnel in my legs; I'll be out of here in a day or two."

"Oh that's great, Joe, I was a little worried. Well I gotta go back now Joe, anything I can do for you before I leave?"

"Yeah, go find me something to drink."

"Joe, where the hell am I going to find you something to drink, we're surrounded and cut off: there are no supplies coming in here."

"Look in one of the taverns."

"Joe, the taverns are all bombed to shit."

"Go look anyway."

"Okay, but don't be surprised if I don't come back."

I walked out of the church and down the street. There was a bombed out tavern on the right-hand side. I went in; everything was broken glass and shattered furniture. No good. I went farther down the street into another tavern. This one still had the remnants of a bar and I was shocked when I pulled the beer handle and beer streamed out. I looked around—no containers of any kind. I took off my helmet, the same helmet I used in my foxhole when I can't get out to the latrine, swished some snow around in it, and filled it up with beer. I went back to the church.

"Hey Joe, I got some beer."

"Holy shit, gimme some of that." Joe sat up and I held my helmet up to his lips.

"Hey, give me some of that." (from one side).

"Hey, me too, gimme some of that."

"Over here."

My helmet was soon empty.

"I got no more."

"Go get some more."

Dutifully I exited the church and went back down to the tavern. I filled up my helmet and started back to the church. When I got to the church, standing in the doorway with his arms folded was the regimental surgeon, a major.

"What the hell do you think you're doing, soldier?"

"Err, ah…Giving aid and comfort to the wounded, Sir?"

"You stupid jackass, don't you know I have chest cases and stomach cases in there, that if you give them beer you'll kill them? Get out of here before I have you shot."

"Yes, Sir."

"And put that helmet on."

"Yes, Sir."

I threw the helmet on my head, beer pouring all over me, and ran like hell before he changed his mind.

End of story, right? No; later events proved otherwise.

The bad weather continued, foggy clouded days and snowy nights. It meant no air support, no food, and ammunition was getting real low. The German attacks were relentless, day and night probing all parts of the perimeter. But the 101st continued to tell them to go to hell. In fact, when the Germans sent a delegation under a white flag of truce asking us to surrender, Gen. McAuliffe's reply was, "NUTS!"

One night I was walking back to our Company HQ from Regiment, having been sent for some maps. We had been told to watch out for German patrols behind our lines in white snow capes (we didn't have any) who were probing for information about any weak spots in our lines. There must have been a full moon. With everything snow-covered, it was almost like daylight outside. I could see my shadow. The wind was blowing hard, whipping up the snow. As I was walking along the road, out of the corner of my eye I saw five white shapes gradually sink to the ground in the open field. My heart jumped.

There was an overturned jeep in the ditch on my right. I pretended not to see them and continued walking to the jeep. Slipping behind the jeep I put down my maps, leaned over the upturned wheels with my M-1, and hollered just once as loud as I could, "Klondike!"—the password for the evening. No answer.

Bang, bang, bang, bang, bang, bang, bang, bang!

Four of them stayed on the ground; one got up, shot at me one time, and ran into the woods. My eight round clip was empty; no more ammo. I picked up the maps and ran like hell. When I got back to the company headquarters, I told the lieutenant about it. He said he'd send someone out to investigate it. "If it's true," he said, "I'm going to write you up for that one."

I never heard anything more about the incident but, about a year after the war, the War Department sent me a letter, a Bronze Star Medal, and a commendation signed by my company commander for "meritorious achievement in ground operations against the enemy in the Ardennes." I wear that medal proudly today.

Another incident...the luckiest cow in Bastogne. It was the fourth or fifth day of the battle and we were being shifted around again to meet different points of attack. We were two squads of H Company in an old barn somewhere near Mont, waiting to move out to a new position. It was just about dawn. Looking out the dirty barn window, I can't believe my eyes. It's a skinny looking cow in the barbed wire yard enclosure, but all I can see is a sizzling steak on that stove here in the barn. Screw that stupid K-ration I have in my pocket.

"Hey you guys, would any of you know what to do to make steaks out of that old cow?"

"Sure," said Louie Martin, "ain't nothing different than butchering up a deer during deer season."

"Fantastic, Lou." I hand him the .45 pistol I had, "Go kill that cow and I'll get a fire started." Minutes later, still no shot heard, Lou came walking back into the barn and said, "Get somebody else."

"What the hell is the matter with you," I asked. I got no answer.

"Howard, go kill that cow."

Howard went out there, no shot, and came back in. "You do it."

I take back my .45, walked toward the door, and threw back over my shoulder, "You jackasses make me laugh. You kill men all day long but you won't kill a cow."

I walked over to the corner of the enclosure, noticing how that cow seemed to be all skin and bones; most pitiful looking. I put the gun to her head. She turned her skinny head toward me, looked me square in the face with those big brown liquid filled eyes, and plaintively uttered, not "mooooo," but "maaaaa." I swear it sounded just like she was calling her Mama.

We ate K-rations that day. I guess no matter how tough we think we are, there's a streak of compassion in all of us which sometimes comes out in the strangest of circumstances.

Morale was still high but we were beginning to get a little concerned about ammunition. I later found out that by 23 December, our artillery was down to two shells per day per gun. I myself had one eight round clip left for my rifle and none for my machine gun.

35 A and B. German propaganda leaflet (two sides) fired by artillery shell into the American lines on Christmas Eve.

German propaganda leaflet later used by Vince and his buddies for personal hygiene in Bastogne

Vince after the siege of Bastogne—the "kid" had become a man.

9. RELIEF

DECEMBER 23 WAS A BANNER DAY. UNBELIEVABLY, THAT MORNING THE sun came out. And then, zooming down out of a clear blue sky came six American P-47 Thunderbolts. The nacelles on those planes were painted red, yellow, and blue. They dove down and strafed and bombed all around us. I'll never forget that sight. Some of us jumped up and down like school children at Christmas. "Give it to 'em. Beat the shit out of them. Slaughter them!" Some of us were laughing out loud, others were just staring mute at the puffs of orange and black smoke that arose right after the planes had pulled up from the dive.

And then the most glorious sight of all...over 100 C47's loaded with food and ammunition started dropping parachute bundles, 95% of which landed in our area. Oh joy. Oh happiness, no more worries about taking the war to the enemy. Only one disappointment; there was no winter clothing. Whatever we had, had to continue to do the job of staving off the worst winter in Europe.

One of the most important results of that parachute drop was that the parachutes were immediately taken to the seminary and the church to wrap the wounded in. It was gratifying for us to know that at least the wounded guys were now warm.

Now let them come, the bastards.

The rumor was that Patton was on his way and that he might get to us by Christmas. It didn't happen, but on the next day, 26 December, riding on the third tank, with a scowl on his face, his two pearl-handled six shooters on his hips, his lacquered helmet on his head, rode the General. How we loved it.

The corridor he opened into Bastogne enabled us to get the wounded out to a field hospital and proper treatment, and, we thought, a way for us to get out and back to a base camp for some rest, rehabilitation, decent food, and warm clothing. General Eisenhower had other ideas.

The 101st and 82nd Airborne Divisions were to be the spearhead for kicking the retreating German armies back into Germany. So now the fighting really began as we went on the offensive. The fight for Bastogne was over, but the fight to eliminate the Bulge was just beginning.

At about this time, I began to notice a language change. Slowly but surely I was adapting to the "old veterans" talk. You no longer said just plain "yes" or "no," it was "fuckin' ay" and "fuck no." A simple sentence like, "That bastard just had to raise his head one more time and I'd a put a bullet right between his eyes," became, "That fuckin' bastard just had to raise his fuckin' head one more fuckin' time and I'd a put a fuckin' bullet right between his fuckin' eyes." It seemed like we had no other adjective to describe anything other than "fuck." And everybody spoke that way except the officers. I never heard any of our officers say "fuck" to any of us. Maybe when they were alone they did, but not when we were present. At least that was my experience; others may differ. Maybe that's the meaning of "officer and gentleman."

Then, a certain feeling was beginning to come over me. After you survive the first days of combat, you say to yourself, "Well, I made it this time but surely it can't last, I'm going to get it before long." Now, after surviving for almost four weeks, I began to say to myself, "You know what, I may make it to my twentieth birthday in March. Can you imagine, I'll be 20 years old and still alive?" A feeling that was cut short about 6 January.

At that time, the 501st was beginning to leave the Bastogne area after some real heavy fighting in the Bois Jacques Woods. That morning a sudden mortar attack caught me outside my foxhole. A loud noise, concussion, and then a terrible burning sensation on my right side from my head to my hip. All I remember after that was Steve Pentek pulling me down into the hole we shared, and me trying to put the top half of my right ear back into place. Then a medic pumped me full of morphine and I was in "Lala land" from then on. I remembered little of the bumpy ride on a jeep stretcher back to the aid station, barely hearing a doctor or medic saying, "The piece under the right eye may be touching the brain, we better ship him off to England."

Then more "Lala land" and finally coming to full consciousness in a beautiful clean white bed in a British hospital and a doctor saying to me, "Soldier, I've got good news and bad news. The piece of shrapnel under your eye was not touching the brain and we removed it. We sewed the top of your ear back on and it's just fine. You have no other problems so you should be out of here in about another week. The bad news is, after a seven-day recuperation leave, you'll be going back to your unit."

"There's no bad news there, Doc. That suits me just fine."

10. LET'S HAVE SOME FUN

THE PRETTY NURSE CHANGING THE DRESSING ON MY EAR CASUALLY DROPS a bombshell on me. "You know there's another one of your boys on the third-floor, another naughty paratrooper. He said he was from the 501st Regiment of the 101st Airborne Division."

My heart jumped. Could it be that Joe Willis who had gotten hit again right after he came back to the outfit in Bastogne and was sent to a British hospital? "Is his name Joe Willis?" I asked incredulously.

"I think that's what it is." she answered, "He's from Florida." Damned right that's Joe!

"Can I go see him?"

"No, but he can come up to see you; he's about ready for discharge."

"Please tell him to come up right away; I'm dying to see him."

Sure enough, next morning it's Joe Willis.

"Joe, you son-of-a-bitch. You look great. Are they going to send you home or back to the outfit?"

"I don't know what they have in mind, but when I leave here I'm going back to the outfit; you too, right?"

"Yeah, Joe, but we get a seven-day recuperation leave first. Let's make sure we get discharged at the same time so we can take our leave together."

"Where do you want to go? They said we could go anyplace in the United Kingdom."

"I say Scotland, there won't be too many GIs up there."

"Agreed, we'll put in for Edinburgh, Scotland."

It took some maneuvering but we managed to be discharged from the hospital at the same time. We received our back pay, back rations with a lot of extra cartons of cigarettes from a friendly sergeant, and two copies of our travel orders to Edinburgh Scotland: one copy to be used to convert money, and the other to act as our identification and pass.

And now the fun began. You talk about two scheming, wily, conniving, combat men getting ready to live it up, knowing they were going back to the war in seven days.

We went to the Red Cross and Joe typed five more copies of our travel orders. I signed Captain Hiltons' name to them. At that time on the black market in London, you could get three to one for American money and two to one for British money. So we would go to any bus station or airport or railroad station, convert our money to American or British pounds, double and triple it on the black market, turning in a copy of our travel orders at each place. We ended up with $1200, a fortune in 1944.

The Army was paying for our travel to Edinburgh; we pocketed the money and went to the nearest American airport and asked if they had a plane going to Edinburgh. The American Eighth Air Force stationed there couldn't do enough for us. "Sure we have, Trooper. When do you want to leave?"

"Any time," we said. We couldn't believe they had a C47 supply transport going to Edinburgh within the hour.

When we arrived in Edinburgh, instead of reporting to the Rainbow Hotel on Princes Street, reserved by the Army for convalescing American troops, we pocketed the seven fifty a night the Army gave us and went to the Red Cross instead. At the Red Cross we obtained a room for fifty cents a night.

"Now, said Joe, "we gotta find some transportation. Let's go buy a car." Audacious? Hell no, we had the money. We took a taxi to the nearest car lot and asked what they had for an automobile. They had only one car on the lot that was running and they wanted one hundred pounds for it—about $400 at that time. We said we'd take it. It was a Saloon, the kind of car where the driver sits out in the open and the passenger compartment has curtains at the windows, flower vases on the walls, and carpeted floors inside.

The owner hesitated and then said, "I would really like to sell it to you lads but there'd be no way that you could get petrol for it. Unless you're a British subject you cannot get a petrol ration book." Sobered by that thought, we decided against buying the car.

We called a taxi driver over to us. "How much do you make a week," I asked him.

"Ah, I pull down about two quid (pounds) a week," he said.

"You're full of crap," we answered, "you're lucky if you make 10 shillings, but we'll give you 10 quid a week if you just have your cab waiting for us day and night in front of the Red Cross."

"Righto, Righto," (he was a cockney), the delighted man responded. "At your service, Yanks."

As soon as we settled into our room, with transportation waiting at the door, Joe said, "Now there's one more thing we have to do. We've got to go find something to drink."

Well now, that was easier said than done. You could buy a drink at the local pub, but you couldn't buy a bottle of whiskey anyplace. It was all rationed and only officers received a ration book. We talked to various bartenders about selling us a bottle, willing to pay a very inflated price for it, but no go.

"I say, Laddies," one Scotsman said to us, "you might try the Johnny Walker factory down by the Clyde River. They don't normally sell any of their whiskey to the public, but if you talk to the night watchman, you might get lucky."

Well, Joe and I filled our musette bags with cartons of cigarettes from all the back rations we received and headed out to the Johnny Walker factory. We were told to wait until after dark, which is what we did. As we approached the factory, the night watchman came out to meet us and before we could say a word, he said, "I know what you're after Laddies but I canna help you. It's all rationed and accounted for."

"We know," we said. "We just came to say hello; heard you were a combat man and thought maybe we could have a little chat." We placed two cartons of cigarettes on the table.

"Paratroopers are you? I was in the Black Watch myself, got it in North Africa."

"Wow," we said, "Tell us, was the German Afrika Corps really that tough in North Africa?" We slipped two more cartons of cigarettes on the table.

"Gentleman, you're tempting me and tempting me but I canna do it; it's all rationed and accounted for, each case is numbered on a manifest."

"We know," we said. "But maybe there's a broken case somewhere." I placed my last carton of cigarettes on the table. He looked at it.

"Chesterfields," he said, "my one and only favorite cigarette, let me see what I can do."

He came back out with a whole carton of Johnny Walker Red Label Scotch - twelve bottles! He started to open it, Joe threw his last carton of cigarettes on the table and said, "Don't bother; we'll open it at the house." We picked up the carton before there could be any protest, and left.

We were swimming in gold. Twelve bottles of Johnny Walker scotch. Unheard of. Unavailable. Unbelievable. We retired to the Red Cross, took one bottle out, put the rest under the bed, and proceeded to drink ourselves silly. We went to bed early that night, vowing to do it right the next day.

The second day we had our uniforms pressed, shaved carefully, dressed properly, and asked our private transportation to take us to the nicest restaurant in town. He took us to the Brown Derby in the heart of town. It had a string orchestra playing beautiful music; it had lots of beautiful women as well as servicemen of all nations who all turned from what they were doing and riveted their eyes on us as we placed a full bottle of Johnny Walker Scotch in the middle of our table.

There wasn't much in the way of food choice so we ordered a salad and then proceeded to drink, being watched carefully by the other people there. After glancing at a table with two pretty girls who were smiling at us, we invited them over. Without hesitation, they joined us. I don't know if all the Scot ladies can drink Johnny Walker like that, but these two were certainly good at it. We had a wonderful evening. After dinner, we took the ladies to a dance hall they pointed out, and after stopping by the Red Cross for another bottle, we proceeded to have another party. By this time Joe and I were feeling pretty good. There were a lot of Scot soldiers there in their kilts.

"Vince," Joe says, "what does a Scotsman really wear under his kilt?"

"I don't know," I said.

"Why don't you go find out," Joe said.

"Yeah," I said.

I looked around, picked out the smallest Scot I could find, and foolishly went over to him and lifted his skirt.

"Hey Joe, noth…wham, he hit me so hard I went sliding across the floor and under the table. He came chasing right after me and picked me up off the floor, all apologies.

"I didn't want to do that Yank, but you don't do that to a Scot."

"I know," I said ruefully, "that was a rotten thing to do and I hope you will forgive me and have a drink with us."

"Aye, that I will," he said, "you're the fellows with the Johnny Walker."

"Absolutely right," I said, pouring him a good stiff shot. We then proceeded to toast everyone and everything. We sent for another bottle and invited more Scots to our table. We began to sing, *It's a long way to Tipperary*, *Auld Lang Syne*, the paratroop song, *I Belong to Glasgow*, and so forth. What a wonderful night. The third and fourth nights went the same way.

Two nights left and only four bottles of Johnny Walker remained. Rationing became necessary. One standout thing that I remember about the last night was a Scot soldier coming up to our table and saying, "I know a good joke; if I make you laugh, will that earn me a drink?"

"Sure," we said.

He sat down and proceeded to tell us about Johnny and Jeannie. It was winter time and Johnny and Jeannie decided to get married on Christmas day. In honor of the occasion, Johnnie decided he would make himself a new kilt. He went down to the village shop and announced, "McDougall, I'm inclined to buy three yards of material for a new kilt."

"Johnny boy, you're in rare luck, I happen to have three and a half yards left on a bolt that I will give you at a bargain price."

"I don't need three and a half yards, McDougall, I only need three. What would I do with the extra half a yard?"

"You could always make a scarf for your wife-to-be, Jeannie."

"A scarf you say? A bargain price you say? A _real_ bargain price?"

"Yes, a real bargain price."

"Aye, it's a deal," said Johnny.

Johnny went home, cuts off the half a yard for the scarf, and wraps the beautiful cloth around his waist. "I just have to show this to my girlfriend Jeannie," he said. He tucked in his temporary kilt, threw on his overcoat, and walked the windswept road to Jeannie's house. Unfortunately, unknown to him, the temporary kilt fell off. Knocking on his girlfriend's door, he shouts, "Jeannie girl, come see what I have." Annoyed, Jeannie girl said, "You know its bad luck to see the bride ere the wedding."

"I know," he said, "but there's something I must show you before the wedding."

"Oh all right," said Jeannie and came to the door. When she opened the door, Johnny threw open his overcoat, and said, "Well, how do you like it lass?"

Jeannie gulped and said, "Well, it's…it's nice."

"That's not the half of it," said Johnny. "I've got another half a yard at home to wrap around your neck."

The man got his drink.

As all good things must end, this fun filled week ended and Joe and I made ready to go back to the outfit. We were supposed to report to some American replacement depot in London.

Like hell; reassignment officers have been known to send recuperated soldiers anyplace they wanted to. We went right back to the airport, hitched a ride to France, started asking around as to where the 501st was, and joined them in Alsace-Lorraine, just in time for another good fight. We were back in the war, but oh what stories we had to tell the boys.

In about the middle of March, the whole division was brought back to camp Mourmalon to receive the presidential unit citation.

Joe Willis and Vince invade Scotland

11. BACK IN THE SADDLE AGAIN

I FELT LIKE AN OLD VETERAN NOW, ONE OF THE" BAD BOYS" OF THE AIR-
borne. We still felt like we were going to "get it" before the war was over,
but Bastogne proved to be the death knell of the German Army. It had
used up all its reserves and was now limping back toward Berlin. We had
cut them up pretty badly. So secretly now, in our hearts, we began to
wonder. Is it possible we will be alive for a little longer? Maybe even long
enough to survive the war.

And now for another one of those war-time "momentous occasions"...I
lost my virginity. Surprised?
Listening to everyone in the outfit speaking, I was struck by all the
conversations about women. They all acted like they were old hands
about sex and I pretended to be as well. But the embarrassing truth was,
up until March 1945, I was a virgin. I came close when I first got to
England, even closer when Joe and I were in Scotland, but I had never
quite made it. After my first combat I decided that I was not going to die
never having known the pleasures of a woman. So right after Eisenhower
presented our Division with the presidential unit citation, and we were
allowed passes, I was determined to remedy that situation.
I wrangled a pass to Paris, turned down all offers of companions,
and went alone. Armed with plenty of money and countless stories
from my friends as to how to go about it, I went to the best hotel
I could find in Paris. In the lobby, I waited till he was alone and
then approached the concierge. I asked for a room. As he was doing
the paperwork, I, trying to act like a man of the world, asked about
female companionship. He said that could be arranged. I told him I
wanted only the best and must have started blushing because the old
man, with a knowing smile on his face, said, "Monsieur, is it possible
that this is your first time?"

Shamefacedly, I admitted it. "Oh Monsieur," he said. "They will fight over you."

I blushed some more, took my key, and trying to regain some dignity, said in a casual voice, "Send her up in about an hour."

I went up to my room, took a shower, brushed my teeth, had a drink, and waited that torturous hour. An almost timid knock at the door, and when I opened it, a gorgeous, shapely, blonde, young lady smiled a knowing smile at me. "Oh, M." she said. "We are going to have a wonderful time."

Believe it or not I said nothing, and sat down with my hands in my lap. She came over to me, took my hat off, and kissed me tenderly. She then took off her coat and jacket, stood there in a beautiful black shiny dress, and sweetly asked if I had anything to drink. As the concierge had instructed me, I handed her the Fr.500 note (about $20 then) and proceeded to pour her a drink.

She went to the bathroom and came out in a négligée that took my breath away. She then said, "M. place yourself entirely in my hands," and proceeded to undress me. I was going crazy, while she continued to smile and kiss me all over. She walked me over to the bed, took off the rest of her clothes and mine, and the next thirty minutes are an explosive haze of never to be forgotten ecstasy.

With snatches of sleep in between, we did that two more times that night, and with that emptying of everything I had been saving up for 19 years, I became a lover of sex. What a night! And what an addiction. After that experience, I seized on every opportunity to make love to a woman; and, in wartime Europe, there was plenty of opportunity. Oh how the innocent have fallen. Blame the War.

For the next few weeks, we finally got a little rest, rehabilitation, and replacements. We and the 82nd airborne were stationed close enough to Rheims to make it our "city of enjoyment." You can imagine what it was like for the people there when you turn out two divisions of paratroopers, recently freed from the tensions of combat, seeking wine, women, and song.

Sometimes, with good cause we thought, we tore up the town a little. Of course the 101st blamed the 82nd, and the 82nd blamed the 101st. Woe to the MPs that tried to tame us. We all knew we would be going back into combat soon and really didn't give a damn. The solution that the High Command decided upon was to permit only one Division at a time to be on pass. Furthermore, they decided to make us patrol ourselves and, when each division was in town, it had to provide its own MPs. What a joke. Did they really expect us, when we were on MP duty, to arrest our own, or to break up a fight if our guys were doing okay?

One night Joe Willis and I were on MP duty in the red light district of Rheims. We hated it. We had an MP armband, .45 pistol, and a billy-club. We decided to have some fun.

The whorehouses were supposed to be off-limits, but we knew that in the higher-class ones officers especially paid no attention to the "off limits" sign (rear echelon officers that is).

We selected one of the better places and went charging in the door with pistols drawn. "Don't anybody move."

Inside the sitting room, bedlam as several officers seated there tried to get up to leave. We said, "Don't anybody move."

Now they didn't know what to do. One of them attempted to pull rank and said, "Listen soldier, I'm giving you an order…"

That's as far as he got, Joe put the pistol up to his head and said, "Unless you want a bullet between the eyes, sit down!"

The officer wilted. They were probably all thinking along the same lines… *These are crazy combat paratroopers and they probably mean it.*

The talk then became entreaty, "You're right, soldier. We shouldn't be here, but you know how it is."

At about that time, the Madame appeared in the doorway, horrified. Joe said in a loud voice, "You're all under arrest. And you, Madame, and all your girls are going to jail."

Cries, sobs, and more entreaty.

Joe and I went into a huddle. Well okay, let's let the soldiers go.

"All right. All you men, get out of here and don't ever come back, off-limits means off-limits to everyone."

There was a rush for the door.

"As for you, Madame, line up your girls."

A torrent of French, then English.

"Oh please, M., we are only trying to make a living. Don't arrest us. We will put a "closed" sign on the door." She places a "closed" sign on the outside of the door. "See, no more."

The girls were lined up.

Joe and I went into a huddle.

"I'll tell you what, Madame, maybe after we relax a little bit with one of your girls, we will decide."

We each take a pretty girl upstairs, have some fun, come back down, take down the "closed" sign, rip it up, and tell her, "It's okay, go back to business."

We walked away with smirks on our faces. What a pair of bastards we were that day. Blame the War.

On the move again. And then, for me at least, the most terrible experience of the entire war. We liberated a concentration camp. I don't remember the exact date, but I believe it was sometime in March or early April. We were aboard the trucks pushing the Germans hard. The trucks stopped outside of a big patch of woods. Here we go again. "All right, fixed bayonets and ten yards apart. We have to clean out that patch of woods. We don't know what's in there, so slow and easy. And look out for mines."

We made a slow sweep through the woods, encountered nothing until we came to a clearing. We noticed a crazy smell that got stronger and stronger until at the clearing it was an overpowering stench. We couldn't believe our eyes!

There was this big compound with two open gates. No Germans were around, but unbelievable numbers of what at one time must have been normal human beings; but now looked like skeletons with skin stretched over them. A big pile of dead in the center, an open pit, and a bulldozer that apparently was abandoned before it finished the job. In the shed-like structures were cubbyholes with a body in each one, some moving and some not. A few were standing, barely able to move, but slowly walking toward us. Others lying prone on the ground were pulling themselves along on their elbows. No talking, only low moans. I stood staring, tightening my grip on my rifle. I felt a rush of hot blood to my head, and then; not fear, not anger, but a feeling of total disgust. How could one man do this to another?

I wanted to lash out in all directions, but was rooted to the spot. Unnoticed while I was staring at this horror scene, one of them had crawled up to me on his elbows and was kissing my dirty boots saying,

"Thank you, thank you." Horrified, I told him to stop and tried to pick him up, but he groaned in pain when I touched him. So I just left him there and took a few paces back. We walked in and saw the ovens, some still smoldering with remnants of bones in them, and shook our heads in disbelief. How could they, how could they! I tried to hide it, but I cried. And then I got so angry I couldn't see. I was looking for Germans, any Germans, anybody that I could vent my anger on.

One man put his arm on my shoulder and started saying something which sounded like, "Magyar Magyar." My buddy Steve Pentek was Hungarian, I asked him to come over and see if he could tell me what this man was saying. Steve spoke to him and the man told him that the little pond out in front of the gates had fish in it. Well we knew what to do about that. We threw a concussion grenade into the pond, all the fish, stunned, came up to the surface and those poor creatures who could still walk, picked up the fish and ate them raw.

An officer came over and told us not to give them anything to eat because it would kill them, they had to be fed food slowly and only certain kinds. Our medics were on the way to do what they could, and we were told to gather outside the compound. We were then sent to search for any enemy that might still be in the area. We found nothing. The German guards had left, but what they had left for us to see, would never be forgotten.

To this day, 70 years later, I can still see that compound, and smell the stench. I can still feel that rush of blood to my head and again want to lash out in all directions but find nothing but stale air to stab at.

We got some grim satisfaction later when we learned that Eisenhower ordered all the people in the nearby town (who claimed to know nothing about it), every man, woman, and child over age 12 to clean up that camp, including burying all of those pitiful looking bodies of the victims. They won't forget that experience for a while.

I marvel that there are some people today who say that the Holocaust was a myth, it never happened. How can they be so naïve when so many of us saw it with our own eyes. For many years, I never spoke of this experience to anyone except 101st Airborne Division men in the 501st who were there. It's painful, even today. I was seriously thinking of leaving the episode out of this book, but how could I? It happened, it's all true, and every now and then we need to be reminded of man's inhumanity to man.

On the trucks again, to a place near Hagenaue, France, dug in near the river, sporadic artillery and mortars, machine gun and rifle fire, but very little movement. You might even call this a relatively quiet sector, but if you raised your head above the foxhole for more than a second or two, you were dead. The Germans were leaving behind some of their best snipers to slow us down. Casualties continued to mount. How we hated to lose so many more men so close to the end of the war.

On the trucks again, northern France, Austria, near the Czech border (first taste of real Pilsner beer; wow), beginning to see German troops surrendering along the autobahn. March and April weather melting the snow and exposing thousands of bodies, beginning to release the awful stench of the dead in war. The U.S. Army grave units were kept very busy trying to get ahead of the situation.

And then the race to Berchtesgaden. We didn't know it was a race until later, but it seems like all units in the area, British, French, and American wanted to get to Hitler's Eagles Nest first. I understand it was the US 3rd Infantry Division that got there first, followed by a small French contingent that got there next, looting the place and venting their desire for revenge after years of Nazi occupation. They got kicked out by our advance patrols. I was with the first batch of 501st men who climbed up all those miserable steps (the elevators had been disabled) and got a good look at the so-called Wolf's Lair of the world's greatest madman.

It had been hit by a bomb, stuff was scattered all over the place, and everybody was trying to pick up a souvenir of some kind. I found two books. One is titled, *Adolph Hitler*, the other *The Third Reich*. Both of them were filled with black and white photos of Hitler and the entire Nazi movement from the early 1930s and 40s. I placed them in my pack and managed to get them home later. They are still in my possession but now on loan to the 101st Airborne Division Museum in Bastogne, Belgium, together with other WWII artifacts that I had sent home during the war. They are on display on the first floor of the museum, together with my original uniform.

There was another thing I saw in the wrecked Eagles Nest that had I had the presence of mind to take it, I would be a millionaire today.

On the wall was a map of the world in three colors as to how the three Axis Powers were going to divide it up. Brown was Germany, red was Japan, and green was Italy. Germany was to get all of Europe down to the Mediterranean, all of the Ukraine and Russia up to the Ural Mountains, and all of the United States and Canada up to the Rockies. Italy was to get all South of the Mediterranean, Africa, and all of South America. Japan was to get all of China and Southeast Asia, India, and the United States and Canada west coast up to the Rockies.

Can you imagine what that Map would be worth today if I had it in my possession? Oh well, win some, lose some.

Lake Hintersei and the town of Berchtesgaden are at the foot of the mountain near the Eagles Nest. When we first arrived at Berchtesgaden, still in combat mode, I saw one of the big Nazi parade banners hanging off the balcony of what I later found out was the mayor's house. It was about eight feet wide by twenty feet long. I decided I wanted that banner for a souvenir. I told the boys in my squad to please hold up for a minute and cover me while I went in that house to get that banner off the balcony.

I fixed the bayonet on my rifle, kicked in the door John Wayne style, and checked for anyone in the room. Nobody; next room, nobody, next room, noise near a big walk-in closet. I opened the doors, and there was a little old fat man, with a little old fat woman, and three little fat kids behind them. He threw up his hands shouting, "Nein Shosien, Nein Shosien."

I motioned them out and said, "I'm not going to shoot you, I just want that banner out there."

There followed a whole chorus of "Nein Shosien's" as the rest of the family joined their father in asking me not to shoot them. Word must've gotten around that American paratroopers had little patience with Germans after they had seen the prison camps. I assured them in a loud voice that I was not going to shoot them and told them that I just wanted that banner. Once convinced, he sent one kid to get the banner, and the rest of them scattered throughout the house bringing me things that they thought I might want as souvenirs. I had to smile at their eagerness to show cooperation. The father kept muttering that they were not really Nazis, they had always opposed Hitler.

It was a funny thing that everywhere we went in Germany we were discovering that there were no Nazis; they were all anti-Hitler, forced by the SS to comply with the dictators of the Third Reich.

I almost felt sorry for them. I picked up my banner and left. I had a few of my friends sign it before I sent it home. More to that story later.

After Berchtesgaden, believe it or not, we were assigned quarters in a German house. For the first time since before Bastogne, we were going to sleep indoors. We couldn't believe it. A bed in a house in the town of Ramseau. What the billet officers did was chase the Germans in the house upstairs, told them that there was a non-fraternization policy in place, and they were not to speak to the Americans nor the Americans to them, under penalty of arrest.

Of course, if the Germans upstairs happened to include a young woman. We just had to speak to her to find out where certain things were in the house, etc. Some of the billeting officers themselves had to look up some of the young ladies for necessary information.

In our German house, Gertrude, whom we called Gertie, caught the eye of Lieutenant Salm. Gertie couldn't help but be friendly to us as we plied her with chocolate and cigarettes.

One day she said to me, "Viencence, vas ist das alles Amerikaner soldaten sprechen, Fug You, Fug Me, Fug This, Fug That?"

We said, (knowing that Lieutenant Salm was coming to see her that evening), "Oh Gertie, that sort of expresses pleasure at seeing someone. But you are mispronouncing it. It's 'fuck you,' said with a smile."

That night a smiling Gertie greets Lieutenant Salm when he arrives and says, "Good Evening, Lieutenant. How are you, I learn good English—fuck you."

We all roared; the lieutenant didn't. He walked away without his date. We had Gertie all to ourselves that evening. Funny thing after that, all the officers really cracked down on the non-fraternization rule. Coincidence I guess.

Another time, and a similar situation with us taking over the downstairs of a house. That morning I'm sitting outside the front door cleaning my rifle when out of the upstairs window I hear a melodious voice singing. I look up and see a nice looking fraulein. She is singing *Lily Marlene* in German. Now, I'm not allowed to talk to her, but then, they didn't say anything about singing, so I responded to her by singing *Lily Marlene* in English. She responds by singing *Lily Marlene* in French. What the hell do I do now? I take out my harmonica and play *Oh Du Leiber Augustine* which is the only German song I know. She laughs out loud and smiles at me. I waved to her to come down. She shakes her head and makes a motion with her hand; nine o'clock (which is after dark).

There! A rendezvous within the law with not a word spoken. We had a lovely evening celebrating the failure of the non-fraternization policy. Blame the War.

April went fast. Hundreds of American bombers and fighters were in the air every day. Germans seemed to be surrendering all over the place. But when the hell was this war going to end? May came on. Some of us were still getting shot at by SS troops who were determined not to surrender.

And then on 8 May it happened. The word spread like wildfire. The Germans had surrendered officially to Eisenhower. The war was over, at least in Europe.

Great God in heaven, some of us had made it, and I was one of them...

12. I SURVIVED!

THE MONTH OF JUNE WAS FUN TIME. WE WERE IN SOUTHERN GERMANY and then in Ober Salzburg billeted in houses and living the good life. Good food, plenty to drink, and women to love, what in hell more would you want out of life.

The bubble burst in July. We learned that, incredibly, the 101st Airborne Division was to be disbanded. What? The best damn division in the whole United States Army? What were they thinking? But it was true. The 82nd Airborne was to be retained in the cutback of airborne units and the 101st was to go. The 501st Regiment was disbanded by the end of July. All the High Point men in both divisions were sent home and the low point men sent to the 82nd Airborne. High Point men were those who were older, married, had children, longer time in the service, or longer combat experience. Deservedly, they were sent home. The younger guys, like me, who were single and had lesser combat experience, were transferred to the 82nd. I was assigned to D company, 504th Regiment. And then the bombshell.

Rumor had it that we were to be flown directly from France, to Panama, to Saipan, in preparation for the invasion of Japan. We couldn't believe it. Without even a thirty day furlough home, we were going to be committed to combat again and to most of us, our death. How in hell could we survive another extended combat assignment? We would surely get it this time. The high morale of a few days ago plummeted. We walked around like zombies, shaking our heads and muttering a lot of bad things about the High Command.

Imagine our joyous revival when in early August we learned that the atomic bomb had forced the surrender of Japan. Oh happy day. The world was a bright place once again.

The rest of that summer was fun and games. We still trained, we made a practice jump to retain our jump status, and we wrote letters home telling the folks "all about it" as we were now permitted to do. Never any of the blood and guts part, only whatever we thought were funny stories and how anxious we were to get home. Our folks responded with packages that now reached us with homemade cookies, special foods, and mom's good old recipes. What a time.

All the replacements that were coming in from the States looked up to us with great respect. We now had time to reflect on the past year and wonder about what we did and how we did it. We didn't dwell on it too much until later in our lives, at least I didn't, and then we did some serious wondering. I'll let it go at that.

Some of us even began thinking about what we were going to do after we got home.

My good friend, Joe Zook said, "Hey Vince, what are you going to do when you get home"

"I don't know Joe, I haven't thought about it too much."

"I'll tell you what you do, Vince. Come out to Idaho. We'll go up into the Sawtooth Mountains, camp, fish, hunt, and steal horses for excitement."

"Joe, don't they still hang horse thieves in Idaho?"

"Yeah, but they'll have to catch us first. We'll bring our M1 rifles with us."

"No thanks, Joe. I've had enough shooting for a while."

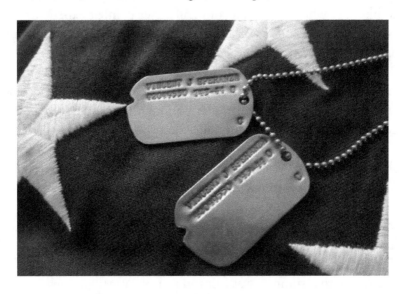

Vince was happy to return with both dog tags

*Practice jump for airborne operations in Asia,
later made unnecessary by the atomic bomb. France, 1945*

First airborne "selfie," 1945

13. COMING HOME

THE NEXT RUMOR WAS THAT AS SOON AS THEY HAD ENOUGH MEN IN EUrope to replace us, we were going home to march in a big parade down Fifth Avenue in New York City, and then be discharged. That was the finest rumor of all. But when?

It took the Army until December 1945, exactly one year from Bastogne, to get us home. Happily, we were told, it would be aboard the Queen Mary which only took four days to get across.

But guess what? Our company commander must've screwed up someplace, because all of D company of the 504th, 82nd Airborne, was assigned KP duty all the way home. I was cleaning pots and pans when we passed the Statue of Liberty coming into New York harbor. Welcome home the hero! The only good thing about the trip home was that we had plenty to eat while on that kitchen duty. Talk about a bummer. A pox on whomever it was from D company that messed up. May you be assigned permanent KP duty in the hereafter.

When I finally did get on deck in full battle gear, I almost groaned with pleasure hearing the cheering crowds as our ship pulled toward the dock. We were home. Not only home, but in New York City, 150 minutes from my house and a dish of real spaghetti and meatballs almost within reach.

Not so fast; we were put aboard trains and taken to good old Camp Shanks, New York. As soon as we settled in, a whole bunch of us who were from New York City asked for an overnight pass to see our folks. No! No! No! No passes until after the parade.

"When is the parade?"

"Not until January."

"Screw you and the horse you rode in on!"

We all went home. We came back in time for the parade, of course, but were threatened with all kinds of courts-martial, summary courts, firing squads, and all kinds of horror including being forced to stay in the Army an extra six months.

Of course nothing really happened; we were to be discharged within the next thirty days. We all marched proudly in the parade then sat around waiting for the machinery to grind out our discharge papers.

While we were waiting they allowed passes into New York City. A lot of my friends, mostly country boys, kept prevailing on me to accompany them on pass to New York City to see the sights. "Especially," they said, "take us to all those fancy nightclubs with the sexy floor shows that you have been talking about."

"Okay let's go."

We began in Times Square, of course, and looking up at the tall buildings that they were seeing for the first time. The farm boys would exclaim, "You can get a lot of baling hay in that barn." Other comments included that those buildings were tall enough to jump off in a parachute.

We stopped in front of Billy Rose's Diamond Horseshoe Bar and Lounge. "Now boys," I said, "this place has a real sexy floor show but I got to tell you, it's expensive as hell."

We counted up all our money, and it was about enough for one beer each in that place. I said, "I'll tell you what we'll do. We'll wait till just before the floor show is coming on, and then we go in, order a beer, and nurse it, understand?"

So, that's what we did. We sat down at a good table near the stage, ordered a beer, and waited for the floor show. I continued to warn everybody to nurse that beer because the waiters will soon be after you asking if you want another drink. And you know New York City waiters; they're very impatient. We talked, nursed, looked around, and kept fending off the waiters. Nothing happened.

"When does the floor show start?"

"Any time now, are you ready for another drink?"

We kept squirming in our seats, pretending to engage in imaginary conversations to keep from drinking from an empty beer bottle. Finally we could stall no more. As we were about to get ready to leave, a man came walking toward us, whom I recognized immediately.

"Hello boys, I wish you to know how much we respect you and what you did for us overseas. I want you to know that all Americans are grateful for your service. Waiter, give these boys anything they want to drink for the rest of the evening and put it on my tab."

"What are you drinking, boys?"

"Er, ah, Scotch," we shouted.

It was Bing Crosby. Needless to say, we sat through two floor shows, drinking scotch and having a hilarious time "on the house." We left the place in "high spirits."

Back to camp.

We were sent to Fort Dix, New Jersey, for final discharge. Fort Dix was the major separation center for the Army on the East Coast. More delays, more paperwork, more fooling around and checking of records, and more plain old bureaucratic nonsense (we thought). Of course it was all necessary in order to do the job right. So we tolerated, and commiserated, and finally with the sewing of the yellow "ruptured duck" symbol of honorable discharge on your uniform, an officer shook your hand, thanked you for your service and sent you home.

At last, at last, at last, we were civilians again. When the finality of that thought sunk in, we began to wonder a little bit. Wouldn't we miss some of the "adventures," the comradeship, the horseplay, and the serious job of taking on the enemy?

Nah. Enough is enough and we were ready for our new lives, unencumbered by anyone telling us what to do all the time.

My family homecoming was riotous; filled with hugs, kisses, pats on the back, laughter, dancing, music, my father's wine, and a massive feast of all the wonderful things that I enjoyed eating. Some wanted to hear me talk about all the things that I had done, others wanted to tell me all the things they had done. I was introduced to the new young members of the family and friends that I had never seen before.

What a wonderful experience. It lasted more than three days. My family had had the extremely good fortune of not losing anyone in the war. Seventeen of the extended family served in the military. Several, including me, were wounded, but none were lost, for which we gave thanks to God in church that Sunday.

It was the end of an era for our family. Now to pick up from where we had left off before the war, to build our new lives in a new world, for the world had surely changed. I looked at pictures of myself of just three years ago, and I couldn't believe that what I saw in the mirror now, was in any way related to that stupid looking kid I saw in the pre-war pictures.

I started to adjust. Number one, I vowed to myself that I would not lay with another woman until marriage. I had gone to confession, and of all the things I had to confess to the priest, the only thing that he said I could do anything about now, was promiscuity. I agreed with him and tried to keep that vow in spite of the many temptations thrown my way.

About a week after my homecoming, I was sitting in the backyard eating a big salami sandwich and having a glass of wine. It was kind of cold, being January, but the sun was shining and I felt good. In the middle of that "feast," I suddenly realized that since my discharge I had not had a serious conversation with myself about my future. I started right then and there.

The first thing I decided was that I was definitely going to get a college education made possible by the G.I. Bill of Rights enacted by the United States Congress. I thought that was the most generous, wonderful thing that my country did for me because I would never have been able to go to college otherwise. What I wanted to do in life required a college education. I wanted to be a school teacher, a high school teacher of American history, and an "expert" in World War II. What I planned on doing was converting the whole world to peace by exposing the horrors of war.

A few years into the profession, I narrowed my ambition to just the United States, and, a few years after that I said to myself, "If one or two kids out of each class per year are really better acquainted with what World War II was all about, I'd be satisfied."

I made a rather unusual choice of college to attend. The G.I. Bill had two parts to it. Public Law 346 was for those of the military who did serve overseas but did not see combat. They were limited to a certain number of months of college based on the number of months they served.

For combat wounded veterans, Public Law 16 enabled them to go to any college that they qualified for and would be carried through to their educational objective provided they stayed in the upper half of the class. In other words...no fooling around. If you were serious about pursuing your career, they would pay for everything and pay you $105 a month for living expenses while in school. How can you beat that? It was a win, win situation. The student got a wonderful college education and the nation had another professional, raising a good family, contributing to the community, and paying taxes.

I therefore had the option to attend any college or university in the US, or even universities in London, Paris, or Rome. I chose none of the above. I chose the college closest to my home on Staten Island; Wagner College. I had had enough of overseas. I wanted to live at home and commute to school.

When I applied, they told me that they were completely filled up and that I would have to wait a year. I agreed to do so because I wanted to go nowhere else away from home.

Now what to do in the meantime? I found our government was not going to repeat the mistakes of World War I where veterans came home to no jobs, and no help. The legislation they passed for us WWII guys included a "readjustment" stipend of $20 per week (not bad money in 1946) for up to three months, while you looked for work. I had my father's aversion to charity. I would have none of it. I went to look for a job.

The Procter & Gamble factory on Staten Island was hiring and gave veterans preference. I went out and signed up. It didn't pay much but it was a job. And what a job!

I was first placed on an assembly line packing Spic & Span Cleaner into cardboard boxes for shipment. I did not last long in that department because every time the machinery came on, it sounded like a machine gun and I would dive for the floor. I asked to be transferred. I was.

They put me on another assembly line shoveling soap onto a conveyor belt to be sent to another part of the factory. One of the advantages of that job was that when you got home you could get into the shower and just rub your chest. You had immediate soap suds all over your body. Easy cleaning. I don't know how long I would've lasted on that job had not the following occurred.

14. A SEAMAN

I WAS WALKING HOME FROM WORK. "HEY, VIN. HOW ARE YOU DOING?"

"Not bad, Frank." (Frank Senerchia, childhood, neighborhood friend) "How about yourself?"

"I'm okay. What are you doing right now?"

"I'm working at P&G; just a fool-around job waiting to get into school," I said.

"Let's go to sea," he said.

"Get the hell out of here. You were in the Navy, but I was in the Army, I don't know anything about the sea."

"You don't have to know anything about the sea for this job. The Army Transport Command is ferrying troops to Europe and they hire civilian crews. Any veteran from any branch of the service gets first choice. Then they give you three months to take the Coast Guard tests and you become a licensed Able-Bodied Seaman. Good food, good pay, and a good healthy life on the open sea. I can teach you anything you need to know to get started."

What a temptation.

"But Frank, I just got home a few weeks ago. My family will go bananas."

"It's not that bad though, Vince. We sail out of the Brooklyn Navy Yard, ten days at sea, three days in foreign port, ten days back, and then one week at home before you go out again. You'll be home one week out of every month."

Man oh man oh man, what temptation.

"Frank, do you think any of those ships would be going to Italy?"

"Sure, any place where American troops are stationed. We will be bringing over the occupation troops and bringing home the veterans."

That did it!

While I was in Europe, I tried so hard to get a pass to visit Rome or

83

any place in Italy. I wanted so badly to see the nation and the people that my parents had come from. But no such luck. Every time my pass to Italy came up, we were being sent somewhere else, or passes were canceled.

I'll do it! Screw the negatives! While I have no wife or family yet, bust out while I can. The only hard part will be Mama, but she'll get over it when she knows I'll be home one week out of every month, and it's only for a year.

Done!

We went to the Coast Guard to get our temporary papers and asked when the next ship would be going to an Italian port. "Don't know and couldn't tell you anyway, the Wartime Secrecy Act is still in force for troopships." So we operated by rumor down on the docks.

"That one, the General M B Stewart, is taking troops to Naples." We signed on.

Bremerhaven, Germany and back.

This went on six more times. Every ship we signed up on went to Germany. I didn't get to see Italy until 1994 when I visited there with my brother Joey.

My first trip to Bremerhaven had an interesting incident. The more I learned about being a sailor, the better I liked it.

We had three days leave in port at Bremerhaven. Frank stayed on board (he was married). I went ashore looking for "action." (I was single and unattached). On a park bench, I spotted a pretty young fraulein who seemed there for obvious reasons. I walked up to her, smiling, and spouted my meager knowledge of her language.

"Gooten tag fraulein, vie gates?"

"Gooden tag mein Herr, So So," she answered.

"Habensei hungar?" (silly question on my part, all Germans were in bad shape for food right after the war).

"Oh, Ja Ja."

I took her to the American Seaman's Club for a nice lunch. After lunch I didn't have to ask; she asked me, "Wilst du mein housa commin?"

"Oh yea, I'd love to come to your house."

It was close by, we walked. We entered the house and to my surprise and great disappointment, a big, tough, typical Aryan looking German was introduced to me as her brother, Hansie. Who the hell wants to meet your brother, Hansie, I mutter under my breath.

"Hello there." We shook hands.

"Wilst du ein bier?" he asked.

"Yea, I'll have a beer, why not."

We each take a pull on the bottle and continue to look at each other. Finally he says, "Vincences, vo bist du in der kreig?" (Where were you in the war?)

"Oh," I answered, "Ich bin eina fallschrimjaeger (parachutist)." His eyes lit up, "Me, too. Ich bin eina fallschrimjaeger!"

"I was with - and I spelled it in the air—101st Airborne Division."

"Ah," he said, "me, German 6th Parachute Regiment (the famous German outfit that we had heard a lot about), we kaputted you in Normandy."

"Bullshit," I said, "we kaputted YOU in Normandy."

He smiled, "Bist du in de Hollande? (Operation Market Garden)

"Sure," I lied, "and we kaputted you in Holland."

"No no," he cried. "We defeated you and the British in Holland."

"Yeah, maybe."

"Bist du in Bastogne?"

"Oh yeah, I was in Bastogne, and not one of you god-damn Nazi bastards ever set one foot in that town even though there were seven Divisions of you trying and only one American Division telling you to "go to hell." So, three times our outfits fought each other.

I think it hit us both at about the same time. We stopped talking and just looked at each other, shaking our heads and thinking. Six months ago we would have been at each other's throats with a bayonet. Today we are sitting here at a table drinking beer. What the hell was that war all about anyway?

Finally he got up, said something to his sister, and walked out the door. She smiled and invited me to her bed. I forgot all about Hansie. It was good. I revised my vow about sex, "once I'm home" changed to "after I'm married."

The next thing that stands out in my "sailor adventures" was the night we were sailing up the English Channel on our way to Bremerhaven. It was dark and stormy, a 75 mile an hour gale we later found out. The masthead light went out. You are never permitted to sail at night without a masthead light. Guess who my "buddy," Bosun Malone, chose to go up the mast and replace the light. The ship was bouncing up and down, water was coming in over the bow, and the mast was shaking like a dog shitting razor blades. Fix bayonets and charge!

I tied a rope around both legs, at the crotch like a parachute harness, then around my waist, and then to a big safety hook. I tied the new masthead light and the spanner wrench to my belt. I believe the mast on those ships was about 40 feet in height (not sure) and has a very narrow steel ladder going up to the top. I took one step at a time, fastening the safety hook to the rung above me each time. The wind was trying to blow me off and damn near succeeded twice but for the safety hook fastened to the ladder. I thought I would never get to the top. When I got to the top, I took the extra piece of rope I had in my pocket and tied myself to the mast because I now needed both hands to loosen the bolts on the old masthead light and replace it with a new one. You talk about crapping in your pants.

I finally got the job done, turned on the new masthead light, and started down just as slowly and carefully as I had gone up. It took a while. The Bosun clapped me on the back, and gave me the next day off. But I still had to play the *Rose of Trollie* for him that night on my harmonica.

The captain of the ship, Captain Olson, sent me a commendation the next day. I really like that. But included in the commendation, was a note asking me to report to him and the first mate on the bridge the next morning at 10 AM. I wondered, what the hell did I do now?

When I appeared the next morning, the captain asked me what my future plans were. I said I wasn't sure yet. He asked me if I would be interested in becoming a merchant marine officer. He said he would sponsor me to the Merchant Marine Academy where I would receive a four-year college education and graduate as an officer in the United States Merchant Marine. I thanked him and asked him to let me think it over for a few days.

I thought about it. An officer in the Merchant Marine makes good money, and has an interesting life in exotic ports all over the world. Good food, a nice warm cabin, and the peace and solitude of the sea. It was tempting but I turned it down. I wanted to become a schoolteacher, a husband, and a father to my children. What kind of a father would I be if I were traveling all over the world most of the time? I never regretted that decision.

Most of my other sea voyages were uneventful. We made unscheduled stops at Southampton, England, once, and the Azores once. In June of that year, a notice was put up on the bulletin board in New York asking for a volunteer crew who would be flown to a Liberty Ship leaving San Francisco for Yokohama, Japan. How tempted I was. I had had some experience in Europe and would love to have had some in the Far East. Good for teaching history. But the ship would not have gotten back home until the end of September and I had to start school September 5. I turned it down. You don't know how happy I am that I made that decision. Otherwise, I would never have met that most wonderful of all human beings—my wife.

It happened this way...

Able-bodied seaman Speranza, 1946

15. MY MAGNIFICENT WOMAN

I RESIGNED FROM THE MERCHANT MARINE IN AUGUST 1947. I WAS AL-
lowed the next 30 days of free hospital care at the Marine Hospital on
Staten Island. I decided I would have a circumcision, seeing as how all
the current sex talk was about a "naked" rather than a "covered" penis
was preferred by the ladies. I reported to the hospital and underwent the
operation. The next morning changed my life.

The ward nurse, trailed by many walking patient volunteers to push
her medical cart, entered the room. I stared at the vision of this gorgeous
woman in her white starched uniform, brunette hair topped by the stiff
nurse's cap with the broad maroon band indicating she was a Registered
Nurse. Her hourglass shape, with beautiful legs (what I could see of
them), an ample bosom, and a winning smile almost took my breath
away. She looked around the room and then straight at me. Oh heavenly
days, is she really walking right toward me? I sat up a little straighter in
my bed, bronzed body, no shirt, egotistical enough to believe my macho-
macho had attracted her. When she reached my bed, she said sternly, "Sir,
hospital regulations require that you wear your pajama top at all times."

I was crushed, my ego shattered, and my face must've shown it because
she gave me a half smile before she left.

What to do now? I put on my pajama top and tried to act the perfect
patient, the epitome of cooperation. I thought up a scheme. I called my
mother, "Mom, when you come to visit me tonight, please bring me a
nice pie or cake or cupcakes; anything homemade."

The next morning, armed with a dozen beautifully decorated cupcakes,
I went to the nurses' station and asked for Ms. Leftwich. "She is off
today," they answered.

I was crushed once more. I was being discharged the next day. The
gods must be angry.

The next morning as I was packing my things to leave, I said to the man in the bed next to me, "Boy, if I get a chance, I am going to date that Miss Leftwich when I get out of here."

"Don't bother," he said. "I've got that all sewed up, she and I have been dating for months now." Again, I felt the pain of failure.

Not being one to ever interfere in other people's relationships, I left the hospital and went home remorseful, sad, and angry with the gods who show you the ultimate beauty and then make it unattainable. I can't blame the war this time, just bad luck. In a few days, I put the episode out of my mind. But it was not to be! Fate would intervene!

It was the end of August; I started school in September, and I was painting my mother's house. I was up on a ladder, it was hot and sticky, and I was singing as I am wont to do on occasions when I am alone and busy. My sister called up from downstairs, "Vinnie, Moki is on the phone (Moki was one of my sailor buddies)." I hated to, but I put my paintbrush in the bucket, climbed down the ladder, and answered the phone.

"Vin, I'm on my way to the Marine Hospital for a check-up, how about meeting me there."

"Moki, I'm painting the house. I'm dirty, hot, and sweaty and would rather finish the job today."

"Come on, Vin, you know I'm uncomfortable around those people (Moki is from Hawaii). Do me a favor. I'll buy you a beer afterwards."

I was about to refuse again, when the thought entered my mind; who knows, I may run into Ms. Leftwich. "Okay, Moki, meet you there in an hour."

"Thanks, Vin."

I showered, shaved carefully, and put on some good looking clothes. While Moki was with the doctors, I sat in the waiting room near the nurses' station. And it happened!

Who should come walking by but that beautiful lady in her white uniform. I stood up and almost stammered, "Hello, how are you? When are you going to let me take you out?"

Her tart reply was, "When are you going to ask me?"

My heart jumped. "Right now. How about this Friday or Saturday night?"

"Friday night will be just fine, pick me up at the nurses' home at seven o'clock."

The rest is history. Years later, she told me that she was so disappointed when she came in to work the next day and found me gone without my even saying goodbye. I told her that the man in the bed next to me told me that he had you "all sewed up" and that you had been dating him for months. She told me he was an unmitigated liar, she had never dated him. He must have been just trying to lessen the competition.

"I had my eye on you from the beginning," she said. "We nurses used to put notes at the bottom of the charts which pointed out certain individuals and their potential, from the doctors' notes they had. Nurse after nurse noted at the bottom of the chart, "Check out the man in bed seven. He's going to college."

I plunged into my studies at Wagner College in September with euphoria beyond belief. There were no problems, nothing was difficult, I got along with everyone. The world was mine because I had its primary jewel, Miss Iva Pearl Leftwich. Oh, what a feeling!

I didn't have any money to speak of so our dates were generally Saturday night at the movies, a hamburger and coffee at the diner, and then long talks in the car parked overlooking the ocean at the foot of Arden Avenue. We later built our home near there. How in the world we could sit in that car and talk for hours and hours fascinated by each other's company, is beyond me, but we did.

I touched her breast once and was immediately given the word. She was a virgin and intended to remain that way until marriage. I never touched her that way again. On Valentine's Day 1948, I asked her to marry me. She accepted and we planned an engagement party for March 23, my birthday. The problem, however, was that I had not yet met her parents and would not even think of an engagement without first requesting her father's permission. We believed in that in those days. So we arranged a trip to Virginia, to her hometown of Vinton.

I began thinking about how I was going to behave. Here I am...a Catholic, a "city slicker," an unemployed college student, and a "foreigner" to boot. The opposite of everything her parents, farm folks from Virginia would probably want for their daughter. But my wartime experiences stood me in good stead. When there's a problem, examine the situation; put the bayonet on the end of your rifle, and charge!

I worried but she had no such qualms. She said that her parents' natural courtesy would make me feel well received and that they would reserve judgment until they got to know me better.

It went as she said. A delightful visit, fruitful conversations, and an acceptance by her father for his daughter's hand in marriage. We drove home completely immersed in happiness.

We had a simple engagement party in March. I gave her the diamond ring, she gave me an engraved silver cigarette lighter for my birthday, and a good time was had by all. The way my entire family treated her belied the problem I thought I was going to have by bringing the first non-Italian woman into the family. My mother and father were so impressed that she was a professional nurse, even to the point of my mother asking for advice on various aches and pains. It was such a pleasure watching these two women, so different, completely engrossed in each other in serious conversation. I was so relieved that they liked each other. As a matter of fact, my wife became my mother's favorite daughter-in-law.

And now, the really big problem. In my day, you did not think of asking a woman to marry you until you had a good job and a place to live. I was a freshman in college living in my mother's home. I did have an income, however, since under Public Law 16 for combat-wounded veterans, a stipend of $105 a month was granted while you were in school. However, the understanding was that she would be a June bride upon my graduation, three long years away.

I continued to work hard on my studies seeing her only on weekends. I couldn't stand it. I threw in Wednesday nights. The longer it went the more time I wanted to spend with her. It got to be almost every night. I would bring my books and try to do a little studying but found myself studying only her beautiful figure. My hormones were raging. It was June of 1948 and I just went absolutely berserk trying to imagine waiting three years for June of 1951. When in doubt, fix the bayonet on the end of your rifle and charge!

I just called her up, told her I wanted to speak with her, and met her at the nurses' home. I told her we should marry in September. I could wait no longer. If I were married, my stipend would increase to $130 a month and with part-time jobs I could be earning $200 a month, which wasn't a bad amount of income at that time. I promised her I would violate my Catholic upbringing and postpone children until I graduated.

She was shocked, annoyed at the thought of having only three months to prepare for her wedding, but, smiling broadly said, "Sure we can."

The next three months were crazy. July and August I put my Merchant Marine skills to work getting a job in the shipyard. I earned the extra thousand dollars needed to pay for the wedding and honeymoon. She went around dealing with bridesmaids, bridal dresses, and all the other "bride concerns."

On September 5, 1948, *we did it.*

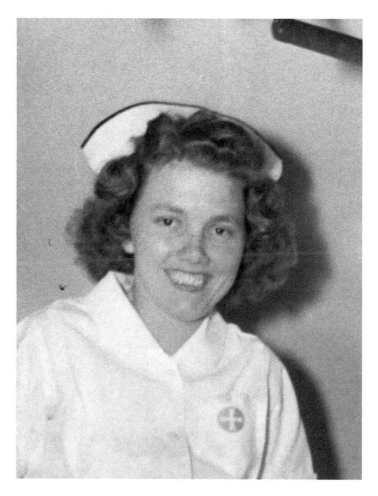

Iva, my nurse, who afterward agreed to
take care of me for the rest of my life.

16. A FAMILY AND A CAREER

WE HAD THE LAST OF THE "FOOTBALL WEDDINGS" IN MY FAMILY. WHEN IT was all over, we drove to Florida for one week of traditional honeymoon. Nothing could have been sweeter. I was now ready to tackle my studies in earnest and begin to take responsibility for the family I was about to create. I doubled up on courses, went to summer school, even went to two colleges at once for a few months (Wagner College and New York University). I received my Bachelor's degree from Wagner in June 1951 and my Master's degree from NYU in September 1951. I completed five years of college work in four.

I looked for a job. No teaching jobs available in New York City, nor was the teachers test (necessary to work in NYC) even being given. I could not fool around; my wife had delivered our first daughter, Susan, in June and was no longer working, as we agreed. I looked on the bulletin board at NYU. "Wanted: high school history teacher, Keesville, New York." Where the hell was Keesville, New York? In the northern part of the state near the Canadian border, just south of Plattsburgh. I discussed it with my wife. She agreed. I applied. I received the position. We packed up the baby and what little furniture we had (a sewing machine and a high chair), and moved to Keesville.

A whole new life in a small town where there were only 450 students in the elementary school, junior high school, and the high school combined. I was the whole history department. What interesting times lay ahead. I was 26 years old, with a wonderful wife and child, and a good job.

I met my first history class with complete confidence. I had paid careful attention to my college instructors, knew how to make a good lesson plan, was a little older and more mature than the average teacher coming out of college at that time, and when I mentioned my wartime experiences, I received instant respect.

Both students and teacher were delighted with each other. I remained in Keesville for just two rewarding years. As soon as I heard New York City was giving the teachers tests again, we moved back to New York, I took the tests, and passed them. I was appointed a substitute teacher at McKee Vocational High School, Staten Island, New York.

In those days, after eight years of elementary school, students were steered into either the academic high schools for the college-bound, or vocational schools for those wishing to learn a trade. The school's recommendations were based on IQ tests. Of course, parents had the final choice. The vocational schools were tough. Most of the low achievers and or non-achievers (who had to stay in school until they were age 16) went to the vocational schools.

It didn't bother me in the least. I found you could be just as effective a teacher by simply teaching more slowly and with more explanations. The important thing is to respect your students. They will return that respect by wishing to achieve for *you* as well as for themselves.

In 1954, I took the requisite examinations for a permanent teacher's license in New York City, passed them, and was appointed teacher of social studies at Tottenville High School on Staten Island.

My high school teaching career was a series of pleasurable days and weeks doing what I loved most; interacting with young people. Twice during the next 18 years, I took and passed the examination for Department Head and Assistant Principal, but when the time came for appointment, I turned it down. I would look in the mirror and say to myself, "Is that what you really want to do, sit behind a desk and fool around with people and paper?"

I would always answer myself, "No, the action is in the classroom. When you shut the door, it's you and the kids, and you can both do great things."

My wife would get a little annoyed, knowing that both of the other positions paid more money and had greater "prestige." I would then quote to her, "Life is but toil, when one gets to love his work, his life is a happy one. Do you want me to come home from work every day an old grouch fussing at you and the kids, or do you want to see me come home happy from work, hugging you and the kids?" Her annoyance would disappear and I stayed happily in the classroom. I loved my work.

The Speranzas: Kathy, Vinnie, Susan, Iva and Vince

Chianti, Provolone and Vince

The Speranza brothers, veterans all. Left to right: Al, Rocky, Vince and Joe

Iva and Vince, 25th wedding anniversary

Vincent and Iva Speranza celebrated their 60th wedding anniversary September 5. The couple met at Marine Hospital on Staten Island, New York after Vincent had served in the U.S. Army 101st Airborne Division and where Iva was working as an RN. Speranza and the former Iva Pearl Leftwich of Vinton, Virginia married at St. Michael's Catholic Church on Staten Island in 1948. Mr. Speranza became a high school history teacher while Mrs. Speranza stayed home to raise their three children: Susan (deceased), Vince (wife, Claudia) of Wasilla, Alaska and Kathy (husband, Jim) Wilson of Auburn. They have 10 grandchildren. After living and working in Springfield, Illinois between 1971 and 1980, the couple retired to Florida for 20 years and then settled in Auburn in 2001.

Our 60th wedding anniversary

17. VERMONT

WHEN I WAS A KID DURING THOSE MAGIC YEARS BEFORE AGE 12, MY GOOD friend, Tony Lobat, and I in those glorious summer months of indolent youth used to love to walk to the Port Richmond public library, about a mile and a half away. There we spent hours going through the books in the "youth section," aided by the nice ladies who worked in the library and helped us with our book selections. I became acquainted with an author called Joseph A. Altsheler who had written two series of eight books each. One was called the Civil War series and the other Pioneer Days. The first book in the Pioneer Days was entitled "the forest runners."

To this day, 80 years later, I still recall the thrill of those pages. I remember the main characters...Henry Ware, Paul Cotter, Solomon Hyde, Jim Ross, and the Wyandotte Indian chief, Timendiquas. Their adventures in the untamed wilderness fired my imagination. With phrases like, "They came upon a jewel of a lake with jumping trout aching to be caught," I found myself saying over and over again, "Oh why was I born 200 years too late?"

Can you just imagine a time when a man could go into the woods with only a Pennsylvania rifle, a Tomahawk, and flint and steel, and go wherever he wants to, do whatever he likes, and claim any piece of land "on the jewel of a Lake" for his own. I always wanted part of that childhood dream, the part about "a jewel of a lake."

By 1959, my children were now, Susan 8, Vinnie 5, and Kathy 2. I began to worry about "hot summers" in New York. New York City was a pretty tough place for kids during the summer vacation. Although we lived in a good neighborhood, it seemed so easy for kids to get into trouble. I was determined to do something about it. What I had in mind was trying to buy a small piece of property on a lake or river, put an old trailer on it, and spend summers with the family at our private "resort." I had no idea what lakefront property cost. I figured that some old farmer whose land bordered a lake or river would be willing to sell 50 feet of frontage for $500 or $600. A couple hundred bucks for an old beat-up trailer and I would be in business.

I decided to do it methodically.

With a compass, I drew a circle on a map fifty miles around New York City. I mimeographed a letter to the local Chambers of Commerce of towns within the circle asking to be put in touch with anyone who had 50 feet of lakefront or riverfront to sell.

Talk about a very rude awakening. The prices were astronomical. I enlarged the circle to 100 miles from New York City, and then to 150 miles. Not only were the prices of lakefront still prohibitive, but many of them also told you what size house you had to build and the minimum size of the lot.

Impossible. I was a poor schoolteacher making just enough to support my family.

One day in the teachers' lunchroom, I was speaking to my friend, Chester Sellitto, telling him about my disappointments in attempting to buy a piece of lakefront. Another fellow teacher, Irv Hyman, sitting at a nearby table overheard the conversation and said, "Vince, probably the last frontier for something like that is Vermont. I have a place up there, not lakefront, but a beautiful spot to spend summers and land prices are still reasonable."

"Irv, how will I go about getting some information?"

"I'll give you the names of the three local newspapers up there. You place an ad in the papers saying you wish to purchase fifty feet of land on a lake."

I did. I received three responses. Only one was worth pursuing. It was on Lake Seymour, probably the most beautiful lake in Vermont.

The old farmer, Mr. Carpenter, wrote to me that he would sell me 60 feet on the lake by 100 feet back for $600. I couldn't believe my eyes. I made arrangements to meet him up there to look at the property. When I arrived and he showed me the land he wanted to sell, I was bitterly disappointed. The lake was beautiful but this particular piece of land had only a few feet of level beach and then rose steeply and was heavily wooded.

I could not believe my chagrin.

Of course, at the time, I did not know what a bulldozer could do and how easily houses could be built to accommodate the property contours. I shook my head and told him I wasn't interested in that.

"Well, Vince, let me show you the rest of the place, maybe you'd like to buy the whole thing. It's 300 feet of lake frontage, by 600 feet back, and it has a house on it."

"No, I'm sure I couldn't afford anything like that."

"Come look anyway."

"OK."

We walked along the edge of the lake and now saw a beautiful spot; a large flat area with a "house" on it. House is not the proper word. It was what the Vermonters called a "camp," an unfinished shell. But it did have running water, electricity, and a flush toilet.

I smiled sadly, because I was sure it was out of my reach. But I asked anyway. "What are you asking for it, Mr. Carpenter?"

"Well, I had it listed for $7500, but you can have it for $5500." I almost fell into the lake.

"$5500?" I inquired incredulously.

"Yep, it's about what I need to start my house in town, I've quit farming."

Now please understand that at this time I did not have a pot to pee in. I had no savings or other assets. It took everything I made to support my family. But tell me, how do you pass up a deal like that?

"Mr. Carpenter, of course I'll have to consult with my wife and family and get back to you. Will you hold that price for me for 90 days?"

"Yes I will Vince, because you seem like just the kind of guy I want to sell this place to; a good family man."

"Excellent, I'll be in touch with you by telephone within the 90 days. Do we have to put anything in writing?"

"No Vince, a handshake will do." I shook his hand firmly, and thanked him.

And now the mad scramble began. Before I left Vermont I went to the local bank. "I need $5500, what's the best you can do for me?"

"You will need $1500 down payment, and then $30 a month for 10 years."

"Excellent, I will get back to you by telephone."

Back home I went over the budget assiduously. All I came up with was $500. I needed another thousand for the down payment. I did not wish to ask the family, both for reasons of pride and the knowledge that none had money to spare anyway. I went to two of my schoolteacher friends, both of whom were bachelors at the time and seemed "well-off."

"Chester, Jules, if you will each loan me $500, I will repay you at the end of the year at 5% interest (the savings banks were paying 3 1/2% interest). No payments in between, just a lump sum repayment at the end of the year."

"Sure, Vince," they said without hesitation.

By the way, when I did repay them, neither one would take the interest. "We wouldn't have done you any favor if we charged you interest, what kind of friends do you think we are?"

I then proceeded to take every part-time job in view. Summer school, evening school, dance chaperone, Wednesday night basketball coach, and Christmas time substitute postman.

I concluded the whole deal over the telephone and in the mail. NOW! NOW!

The Speranza family had a "house" on a lake in beautiful Vermont.

Within three years I had the entire mortgage paid off. From 1963 on, my kids did not know what it was to spend a hot summer in New York. It changed their lives and they still express gratitude to me for it. My wife was ecstatic. I cannot tell you the pure joy and pleasure that we experienced at that place. While I was working, we spent two months up there every single summer. After retirement, we spent five months up there every summer. You cannot believe the beauty of our place in Vermont. Only since my wife has been in the nursing home, have we failed to go to the "Lake House."

An incident that took place in Vermont introduces Uncle Dominick, a man you just have to marvel at.

One evening, Uncle Dominick and I were sitting at the table on the deck overlooking beautiful Lake Seymour as the sun was going down. We had just finished dinner; the ladies were in the kitchen loading the dishwasher (I had modernized my Vermont "camp" into a nice house with a modern kitchen). Uncle Dominick and I were having a last glass of wine. He seemed rather pensive and when I asked him what he was thinking about, he said, "You know, Vinnie, I wish all the people in the world could have it as good as I've had it here in America." He then started telling me the story of his life. I was fascinated.

He was born one of six children in a poverty-stricken village near Bari, Italy in 1892. His parents were overjoyed to hear that a baker in Bari, noting the boy showed promise of intelligence, was willing to take him as a baker's apprentice at the age of seven.

Awakened at 2 AM in the morning, helping to bake the bread, and then delivering it with no wages and not attending school, young Dominick grew to hate it all. At age 14 when his apprenticeship was over, he headed home to tell his parents he was going to America. His parents forbade it, saying he had no one there to help him and besides he had a good trade now enabling him to get a job at home. Young Dominick would have none of it.

When he was 15 he had enough money to buy a one-way ticket, in steerage, and sailed immediately for America. Arriving in New York, no one to meet him, barely able to speak the language, he went to the Catholic Church on the lower East side and asked for help. The good fathers there fed and housed him for a few days and then told him there may be a job for him on the docks.

He went, and was immediately recruited for work in the coal mines of West Virginia. He was paid in scrip money which could only be used in the company store so as to keep you in debt to them and not able to leave. Three weeks on the job and disaster struck—Dominick broke his leg. In those days of no unions, no sick leave, no unemployment benefits or welfare, you were simply fired if you could not do the work. He begged and pleaded with them to let him stay on as a bookkeeper at half pay. They consented.

He learned bookkeeping on the job and stayed long enough for his leg to mend. Returning to New York, energetic and resourceful, Dominick held a variety of jobs, always improving himself. Along the way he married Anna Polizzio and they had three children, Johnny, Francis and Joey. When the two eldest children graduated from high school, Uncle Dominick decreed that Joey, who showed the most promise, would go to college. Therefore all the others in the family would go to work to pay for Joey's education.

So Uncle Dominick, Aunt Anna (he called her Annie), Johnny, and

Frances all went to work as seamstresses in a factory in Ozone Park, Queens, mostly because the factory paid piecework, meaning you were paid not by the hour but by the number of pieces you produced. With hard work you could earn more than the average salary.

Joey went to college, to law school, became a successful lawyer, and then was elected to the Congress of the United States. He was reelected to the House of Representatives every two years for 26 years. Ready to become the chairman of the powerful armed services committee, he died suddenly of liver cancer. They named a bridge after him in Queens: the Joseph P Addabbo Memorial Bridge.

Meanwhile at home, Aunt Anna began suffering from dementia and then Alzheimer's. Though he could have placed her in the finest of nursing homes, Uncle Dominick refused to entrust his "Annie's" care to anyone anywhere except himself. He did everything in the house, and everything required by the doctors for Annie's care, even though she no longer recognized him.

When she finally passed away at home, he made all the funeral arrangements and had her buried at the local cemetery. Within one week of her death, he put all his affairs in order, left half of his considerable estate to their surviving children, the other half to the church on the lower East side that first helped him. He then crawled into bed and died himself. Only in America folks, only in America.

18. A GREAT MAN PASSES AWAY

IN THE LAST YEARS OF MY FATHER'S EMPLOYMENT AT RH MACY & CO. INC., just before retirement, the company doctor informed him that he had diabetes. Hearing about it, my brother Joey and I immediately arranged a doctor's appointment as we felt, if caught early, Pop could avoid its damaging effects. When we arrived at the doctor's office, we found that Pop's regular doctor was not in attendance and that a new, substitute doctor (a much younger man) would do the examination.

Although my father spoke perfect English and understood it well, he always asked the older boys to go with him on doctor's appointments. He said he wanted to be sure of what the doctors were advising and that we would be able to double check on what was being said. After an hour-long examination, the doctor and my father approached us in the waiting room.

"Joey, Vinnie, I want you both to hear what I tell your father so you can help him." He then turned to my father and said, "Mr. Speranza, you have diabetes and you need to make some changes in your daily life. These changes will prolong it.

"Now I know you Italians like your spaghetti sauce but, you must cut it out since it contains too much acid." My father looked at us, frowning.

"And Mr. Speranza, I also know you like your wine; no more." My father looked at us incredulously.

"And also Mr. Speranza, you're a smoker and you have to cut that out as well." My father's look was now out and out rage.

With a choked voice he says to my brother and me, "Andiamo, Andiamo" which, in Italian means, "Let's go, let's go," but if said with a certain look on your face, it means, "Let's get the hell out of here *right now!*"

Outside, my father yelled out loud, "What the hell is he talking about! If a man can't come home from work, have a dish of spaghetti with a glass of wine, and then go smoke a cigarette, who the hell wants to live any longer!" He can go kiss my ass.

And then, he deliberately lit up a cigarette, and blew the smoke at the doctor's office. That's my father.

In the ensuing years, Pop's "diabetes diet" was the joke of the family. Mom couldn't stand just giving him half a glass of wine. She'd pour, look at it, pour more, look at it, and then fill it up anyway. Nobody could stand the thought of us all enjoying a spaghetti dinner while Pop had a dish of vegetables. Mom tried it only once, and it was a disaster.

The even bigger joke was the diabetes testing kit. You urinate into a little jar, add certain chemicals to it, and, if it turns blue, it's good. However if it turns red, it's bad. Well Pop must've been colorblind, because he would proudly come out of the bathroom holding his little jar full of urine which was pinkish, and say, "See how nice and blue?" That went on for only a short while, and then he never showed us anything again, probably because it was always bright red and his diabetes was worsening. He seemed almost spitefully to smoke more. He smoked cigars, cigarettes, a pipe, and now and then, the strongest tobacco product we ever came across, Di Nobile cigars. He still made the best wine in town and continued to enjoy drinking it. Everybody knew that it was going to catch up with him sooner or later, and, in 1963, it did.

His unattended diabetes had overwhelmed him and he was taken to the hospital. The doctors called the family and told us the horrible news that gangrene had set in and they would have to amputate his right leg. Also, his mind was going and we were to expect less coherence when we spoke with him. He had lost so much weight that he was now only a shadow of himself.

They operated. Pop survived the operation and was placed in a nursing home.

A nursing home??? Not Pop.

"Take me home, understand?"

We did. Joey immediately obtained a hospital bed and what other equipment we needed, set it up downstairs near the kitchen, to be easy for mom to get to. We brought him home.

It wasn't long before mom called the family together and said she could not do it alone. Too much was required and she needed help.

We immediately organized a schedule. There were enough of us in the family (eight) so that we would get the "duty" only once a week. Every night one of the eight families would send someone to spend that night and the next morning with Pop. I had Thursday nights. I would try to talk to him, remind him of some of the fun things we used to do, but his mind was wandering in and out of reality and my talk was to no avail. It was sad. I mean really, really sad.

One day in 1964, while I was sitting with him, he suddenly looked at me and in almost a normal voice said, "Vinnie, take me out to the backyard."

"Pop, I can't take you out to the backyard; you have to stay in bed."

"Hey, did you hear what I said to you? Take me out to the backyard, Capice? (understand?)

"But Pop....."

"Now, Vinnie."

I threw a blanket over my shoulder, picked him up like you would a child–he weighed only about 90 pounds with that one leg missing, a shell of that wonderful robust man he once was, and carried him out to the backyard. I put him in his chair near the garden.

And then he gave me the sign. Two fingers to the mouth and back in the motion of puffing on a cigarette.

"Pop, I can't give you a cigarette, the doctors said..."

"Hey, I said, gimme a cigarette, understand?"

Dutifully, I pulled out a pack of Pall Malls, put one in his mouth and lit it. He spent the next few minutes puffing on that cigarette without pause, as though he was afraid I was going to take it away from him. He finished it, handed the stub back to me, and motioned for me to stomp it out on the ground. "Now, take me back to the house."

That night he died. The entire family drowned in their tears.

In 1970, the second disaster that shook our family to the core took place. Mom had passed away. We could not believe that that magnificent Sicilian woman would no longer be with us. She died of lung cancer although she never smoked in her life. If there's a real case to be made for the danger of secondary smoke, Mom was it.

The focus of our entire extended family was now gone. No matter how hard we tried to bring back some of the old days, it was never the same. When big brother Joey called a family council to dispense of our parents few possessions, all I asked for was Mama's 18 inch wooden spoon. I still have it in an honored place in my present home. What smiling memories I have whenever I look at it.

19. THE UNION

NEAR THE END OF MY TEACHING CAREER, IN 1968, A SPURT OF NEW CHAL-
lenges and events provided another twist to my life. I was part of a major
movement; the organization of the teachers of the City of New York into
Local 2 of The United Federation of Teachers AFL-CIO.

The problem had been festering for a long time. School teachers were
underpaid and undervalued. It's hard to imagine in today's world but,
my first job in Keeseville, New York, paid $2,700 per year. That was
only because I had a Master's degree as well as a Bachelor's. Otherwise
the salary was $2,500 a year. Everybody in New York City with just a
high school diploma made more money than that. The first summer in
Keeseville, I got a job parking cars at the Au Sable chasm. In two summer
months, I earned $2,000 in salary and tips; almost as much as I earned in
ten months teaching history to the youth of America. I had a wife and a
child to support and we barely made it. It wasn't right.

When I started working in New York City, it wasn't much better. Each
year we would form a salary committee which, hat in hand, would meet
with the Board of Education and respectfully request raises in salary and a
voice in conditions of employment. The Board would always smile, serve
us tea and cookies, and say that they would take it under advisement.
Nothing ever happened until in the early 1960's when a movement for
collective bargaining began in the high schools.

I was among the first on Staten Island to sign up with the United
Federation of Teachers organization. I was at Curtis High School by
that time and was voted Chapter Chairman (union representative). I
began attending union meetings after school. Our goal was simple.
Since the Board of Education would not pay any attention to us, we
would opt for collective bargaining which, under the law, forced them
to deal with us.

I could go into a whole litany of events here including strikes, firings, mass meetings, and picketing, in the heady days of the 1960's. What we achieved was, first, collective bargaining, and then a negotiated, signed contract. What an improvement in salary and working conditions. It didn't take us long to sign up all 60,000 school teachers of the City of New York. Later we organized all non-teaching personnel for a total of 75,000 members. I don't know what the number is today. We made a big, positive, difference in the lives of school teachers and their students.

In 1970 I was 45 years old, had 20 years in and qualified for a pension collectible at age 55. Two years previous to this, I had become one of the 16 full-time field representatives of the 60,000 member United Federation of Teachers. As the first successful teacher organizers, we were looked to for help by other teacher organizations just getting started in other parts of the country.

My union sent me and my colleague, Joe Pachco, to Los Angeles to help the UTLA (United Teachers Los Angeles) in its first strike. I did a certain kind of job out there and came to the attention of the Illinois Education Association. After I returned home from California, I began receiving phone calls from Illinois offering me positions in their new organization. The pay they offered was only a few thousand dollars more than I was making and I did not wish to relocate for that little improvement. The calls kept coming, upping the ante, until they offered me so much money that it was difficult to refuse. I called my family together (there were five of us now), gave every member a say, and was surprised at the unanimity. Every one of them was ready for a move. Me, I was already qualified for a pension in NYC and ready to move on.

In 1971 we moved to Illinois, built a house in Springfield, and I went to work as field representative for the Springfield Education Association. It didn't take long for me to move up to Assistant Executive Secretary for Field Services statewide. And then the fun began all over again.

As one of the few experienced teacher-representatives in the state, I traveled all over the state setting up workshops, leadership courses, collective bargaining committees, recruitment drives, and public relations courses. Illinois quickly became a teacher-union state although they call themselves Associations, not unions. The only real difference was they were not affiliated with Organized Labor. The National Education Association is an independent union.

After a series of strikes, most school boards in Illinois accepted collective bargaining for teachers. We were achieving our goals of better salaries and working conditions. We also achieved what was more important: respect.

20. FLORIDA

BY 1980 I WAS 55 YEARS OLD AND GETTING READY TO GO BACK TO COL-
lege to become a big-time labor negotiator. Really? Really!

I was now going to start going to college again even though I was
eligible for retirement! Who was I kidding? I just woke up one morning
as if it were a no-brainer; put in my retirement papers; and began to plan
with my wife to move to Florida.

She loved the idea. The kids were all gone, everything was paid for, so
what are we waiting for. We had already envisioned the house we were
going to build on the piece of property that we had bought in Florida
many years ago.

Done.

Our house in Illinois sold very quickly. So quickly we had to put all
of our furniture in storage until the new house was built in Florida. We
drove to Florida with camping equipment and put up a tent on our lot
to begin the process of finding a temporary place to live while our house
was being built. We ended up renting a house just about a quarter of a
mile down the road from our lot and were able to supervise the building
of our home every day (to the builders chagrin). It was a lovely home,
easy to maintain, and very economical to run. We could now turn our
attention to just pure fun living.

Iva was in her glory in the yard and garden. Everything grew well in
Florida and she had the greenest thumb of any woman in town. I began
paying more attention to the world news and began to get involved in
politics. It wasn't long before I became a Republican committeeman,
and then began helping out in state elections. I had given up on the
Democrat Party right after the "Great Society" program showed me the
direction they were headed in.

At one point the Marion County Republican Committee even wanted
me to run for office, but I refused knowing that I would never give up

going to Vermont every summer for at least four or five months which would definitely put me out of the running for public office. I was having more fun backstage.

I had been a scoutmaster beginning in New York City in 1948. I immediately sought a troop in Florida. None were available so I agreed to become an assistant scoutmaster in a troop headed by a most able and pleasant young man named Ludwig Olson. Scouting in Florida was marvelous; hikes in exotic forests with all kinds of beautiful blooming plants, plenty of isolated camping spots, lots of sunny days, and young boys who really convinced you that they enjoyed scouting in the outdoors.

The troop was well disciplined and eager to learn.

Our camping-canoe trips were even more exotic. Cypress trees along the river, tree orchids peeking out from the bark of other trees, beautiful white egrets, turtles sunning on logs, blue herons fishing in the shallows, the thrill of an occasional alligator slipping from the bank into the water, and the ever widening circle of a huge bass jumping back into the water.

However, in order to give the boys different experiences, on occasion we would plan a backpacking trip to Springer Mountain in Georgia which was the beginning of the Appalachian Trail heading north. Here the boys got to climb steep hills and mountains, drink from cold rushing mountain springs, and camp among the oaks and maples of hardwood forests. We all loved it.

I must say that Scouting, as it was then, is one of the finest character building organizations in existence. I hope it is the same today.

Living in Florida also meant getting a lot of company from up North. How family and friends enjoyed a week's vacation at Vince and Iva's house. We set up our home with all kinds of folding beds, sleeper sofas, and convertible couches so that we could accommodate large family groups. Since our family groups were all brought up to be "working guests," the job was never overwhelming. The women all got together to do the cooking, the men set up tables and did the specialty cooking on the grill, and the cleanup. A good time was had by all and no one was overburdened. How we enjoyed it.

Come May, however, all Florida life was forgotten as we headed north to Vermont; a different, wonderful, world entirely.

21. TRAGEDY STRIKES
THE FAMILY

I WAS IN A GUN SHOP IN FLORIDA BUYING A NEW SIGHT FOR MY HUNTING rifle. The very pleasant looking middle-aged woman who was serving me, had a heavy accent.

"Madame," I said, "do I denote a French accent?"

"No," she said, "Belgique"

"Oh," I said, "Belgium."

"Yes" she said, "have you ever been to Belgium?"

"Well yes, but it was during the war and I didn't see anything but bombs, bullets, and snow. I know nothing else of Belgium."

"Oh," she said, "you were in Belgium during the Battle of the Bulge?"

"Yes."

"You were in Bastogne with the 101st Airborne Division?"

"Yes."

"And you have never been back?"

"No."

"Oh, Monsieur, you must go back. The people of Bastogne have never forgotten the 101st Airborne Division. They celebrate the battle every year in December and re-enact it. There are monuments all over the city to the 101st Airborne Division. You must go back! You will be honored. If you go to Bastogne and wear a little pin that says the 101st Airborne Division, you don't buy a drink or a meal the whole time you're there."

Wow, that sounded pretty good to me.

I started thinking about it, but events forced me to put it on hold. It was the year 2000 and my beautiful, wonderful wife, had been diagnosed with Alzheimer's.

In 2001, another stab in the heart. My beautiful, talented 51-year-old daughter, Susan, passed away from cirrhosis of the liver. Her alcoholism finally had its way. In spite of four attempts at rehabilitation, the last one being at the famed Betty Ford Center in California, nothing availed. Thirty years of heartache was replaced by a deep hole in our psyches. My wife's Alzheimer's spared her the pain. I still feel mine.

In 2001, my wife and I were both 75 years old and enjoying life to the fullest, but the Alzheimer's diagnosis put a huge brake on our merry-go-round of love and fun. My entire world was beginning to shrivel as I read and researched the disease that it seems we can do nothing about. The realization that I would lose her in three to five years (the best estimates at that time) devastated me. They told me to put her in a full care nursing home.

"Like hell," I said. "There's nothing they can do for her in a nursing home that I can't do for her right here at home." I began to learn the process of becoming a full-time caregiver. It is a horrible thing to have to watch the slow but inexorable descent of a wonderful human being into a lesser person.

As we could no longer travel to Vermont and accommodate my wife's love of swimming, I built a swimming pool at home. The experts told me that swimming was the finest exercise for older people and that exercise and medication might slow down the deterioration process of Alzheimer's patients. She went in the pool twice, and then would never do it again; for what reason I will never know.

Things got worse. Her incontinence forced me to buy twin beds with rubber sheets and a special mattress. For the first time in sixty years my wife and I slept separately and no longer made love. We were now both eighty and I began to feel as though I was slowly dying with her.

One morning in 2007, when I went to wake her, she would not sit up. She kept slumping back down onto the bed. She would not open her eyes and I panicked. I called 911. They rushed her to the hospital. They later told me that on the way she had had a heart attack and was in a coma when she arrived at the hospital. I went to the hospital and waited. 24 hours later the doctors came out and said that she was reasonably okay but I could no longer take care of her at home. She was to be put in a facility that had 24-hour medical attention and care. It killed me. After seven years of taking care of her myself, I now had to turn her over to someone else.

I cannot begin to describe to you what it was like when I took her to the nursing home to leave her there. She clung tenaciously to my arm, we were both crying, my daughter tried to help, but Iva hung on fiercely. I sat down on her bed with her and gently kissed her while releasing her arm grip. I managed to get away; a wreck of a man. My daughter and I went home and it was not until my daughter left for her house, that the full realization hit me right between the eyes. After sixty years of always having a wonderful companion with me through thick and thin, I was now to be alone. What a miserable, depressing thought.

The doctors told me that I was in very good shape for a man my age—a healthy life and genetic luck. I had a different explanation. God was keeping me alive and well to continue to take care of my wife who was defying all the odds at staying alive for twelve years with Alzheimer's.

I was alive all right, but as the days without her at home continued to slide by, I felt like an old man sitting around waiting only to die. I lived only for the one hour each morning that I visited her. I wasn't really unhappy about that. Hell, I'd lived a long and happy life and was ready to go as soon as she did. It was not to be.

Here I must give my wonderful family, especially my daughter, Kathy, my unreserved praise and thanks. They sucked me into the vortex of their daily, busy lives as though I had been a part-of-the-whole from the beginning. They made me feel like the patriarch of a loyal, devoted family group even though I did not join them until 2001. They bridged that horrible first few months of loneliness by inviting me to all kinds of family functions and activities, treating me with great courtesy and respect. My granddaughters called me a "cool grandpa." I revived my interest in life.

22. SUDDENLY, RENEWAL

ANOTHER BIG CHANGE WAS COMING. I GOT A HINT OF THIS CHANGE IN 2004.

I received an e-mail from a lady named Peggy Moller McCarthy whom I recognized immediately as a former student of mine from Curtis High School. Her e-mail said that the class of 1963 was having its 40th reunion in New York City and would I please attend. I delighted in saying "yes" as it would coincide with a visit to my family on Staten Island.

It was a dinner at the Staten restaurant and how I marveled at seeing all those "kids" that I remembered as 18-year-olds who were now 58-year-old senior citizens. Some I recognized, others had to introduce themselves.

One of the men came up to me and said, "Hello, Mr. Speranza, do you remember me, Buz Altshuler?"

"Give me a hint, Buz," I said. "It's been 40 years."

"I was in your history class, and you can't believe how you inspired me telling us about your experiences in World War II. When I graduated from Curtis High School, I went to West Point, graduated as a lieutenant and became a paratrooper like you. I did two tours in Vietnam, was wounded, promoted to captain and stayed in the service."

"Wow," I exclaimed. "That's great, Buz, I'm glad to hear it. What are you doing now?"

"I'm still in."

"Where are you?"

"I'm at Fort Bragg."

"What do you do there, Buz?" I asked.

"I'm the commanding general of the U.S. Army Civil Affairs and Psychological Operations Command (Airborne), a part of Army Special Operations Command. I want you to come out there as my guest to talk to my young troopers and inspire them the way you inspired me."

What a pleasant, wonderful, surprise!

"Absolutely," I responded. "I'll come out there as soon as I can arrange it."

I went. It was great. I was treated with great courtesy and respect. I stayed at the General's house and it was quite an experience watching a General cook steaks on his grill for a PFC, and still referring to me as Mr. Speranza. I visited both the 82nd Airborne and Airborne and Special OperationsMuseums, the training areas, and was allowed in the briefing room as they discussed Iraq. How great to see all those young fighting men ready for anything.

As I was about to leave, I thanked Buz again, told him how much I enjoyed being with the 82nd Airborne, and then asked about the 101st Airborne. He told me that they were at Fort Campbell, Kentucky. "Why?" he asked. "Would you like to visit there?"

"Yes, very much so," I said.

"Well I can arrange that," he said. "The general there is a good friend of mine, his name is Petreaus. I'll give him a call." A week later, I received an e-mail.

"Dear Vincent Speranza, my good friend, Maj. Gen. Altshuler, has told me that you were his former history teacher, a World War II veteran with the 101st Airborne in Bastogne, and would like to visit Fort Campbell. We would be delighted to have you. I'm a little busy in Iraq right now but my Chief of Staff, Colonel Laufenburg, who is there now, will take good care of you. Please let him know when it is convenient for you to visit."

Another General, treating a PFC, like a VIP. "What hath God wrought?"

If I thought my treatment at Fort Bragg was great, my welcome at Fort Campbell was even greater. A Lieutenant Koop with a car was assigned to me for the whole time I was there. He drove me to my quarters, which were a suite of rooms. He drove me to the enlisted men's mess where I had indicated I wanted to eat. He escorted me throughout the camp to visit the museum, to see the old C-47's we used to jump out of, and to sit in on a briefing for battlefield officers. It was then that I found out that the 101st Airborne was no longer all jumpers. Only one Regiment, the 501st (my old outfit) was still jumpers, but the 502nd and 506th were air assault; helicopters.

He took me to a large field and I watched these tough young men boarding helicopters and rappelling down to the ground. I'd never been in a helicopter. I was busting. I dared to ask, "Would you let an old trooper try that?"

"Oh no sir, they wouldn't permit that, but I could take you to the training towers."

We went to the training towers, 60 foot-high wooden structures with four rappelling ropes hanging down. I watched with envy as those young men ran up the steps and rappelled down to the ground.

"Well, would you at least let me try that?"

"Are you in good shape, sir?" he asked.

"Oh in very good shape (for a 79-year-old I muttered under my breath)."

He hesitated, and then said okay. A young sergeant put a helmet on my head, put the proper ropes around my legs, and handed me a pair of gloves. At the top of the tower, the young sergeant asked me if I had done this before. My answer was, "No, but you're going to show me right?"

"There's nothing to it," he said, "you just pull back on the rope behind your back and it acts like a brake."

"No problem," I said.

Lieutenant Koop was taking pictures of all of this as I rappelled down to the ground to the cheers of all the young men watching this old "grayhead."

His cell phone rang, "This is Colonel Laufenburg, you and Speranza report to my office immediately."

My heart sank. Good God, the lieutenant was going to get in trouble. "Lieutenant," I said, "This was all my idea, you had nothing to do with it, I was the one who insisted."

When we arrived at Colonel Laufenburg's office, there stood the colonel, a bunch of other officers, and a photographer. As soon as I walked into the office and was introduced to the colonel, I told him that the whole affair was my doing and that I hoped he would forgive me if I had done anything wrong.

"Now wait a minute," he said, "what I heard is that you rappelled down our training tower."

"Yes sir, but it was I who insisted on doing it, and Lieutenant Koop is not responsible."

"Just a minute, Speranza, there's nothing really wrong. In fact, we believe that your action makes you an honorary air assault soldier." And he pinned a pair of air assault wings on my jacket, gave me a big hug, and a salute. How I loved that man at that moment.

"Thank you, sir," I blurbed, trying not to get emotional. "And may I say that Lieutenant Koop has been a most cordial, helpful, and informative escort."

I left Fort Campbell full of love for the human race.

It was 2009. I tried to keep myself occupied by getting involved in community affairs. I became commander of the Veterans of Foreign Wars in our town. Being involved in Veterans Affairs, brought back the thought of that woman in Florida telling me about Bastogne. Now that I had the time, and no caregiver duties at home, maybe I would go back just one time and visit the battlefields, or more importantly, the cemeteries where I would pay my respects to my fallen comrades, long neglected.

Vince observes air assault Operations at Fort Campbell, home of the 101st Airborne/Air Assault Division.

Vince—at age 79—negotiates the 60-foot rappel tower at the U.S. Army Air Assault School, Ft Campbell, KY.

Vince is made an honorary Air Assault Soldier by COL Laufenberg, 101st Airborne Division chief of staff.

23. OVERSEAS AGAIN AFTER 65 YEARS

MAYBE IT WAS THE SERIES OF MOVIES LIKE *D-Day, Sixth of June, Saving Pvt. Ryan,* and *Band of Brothers* that awakened interest in World War II. It seemed like people went out of their way to speak to us World War II vets and listen to what we had to say. They started calling us the greatest generation, and heroes.

Maybe I'll go back just for the hell of it. It's been 65 years since I left Europe. What would I find? When I mentioned it to the family, the cries went up. "Pop, you're 84 years old; you shouldn't be traveling around Europe by yourself."

"Okay," I said, "then one of you come with me."

They hemmed and hawed about who could get the time off from work, and it was finally decided that my daughter, Kathy, would come with me. "That being the case," I said, "we'll only spend three days in Bastogne and I'll take you to Paris for three days." (Kathy had never been out of the country.)

That suited everyone just fine. Jim Wilson, my son-in-law, made all the arrangements on the internet. I had no particular game plan and I had no contacts there. I had heard that there was a museum in the center of town (Bastogne) that had maps and other information about the 101st Airborne Division. My thought was to hire a taxi, ask to be taken to the outskirts of town, and look around to see if I recognized anything.

A chance meeting changed everything.

We were booked at the Leo Hotel in the center of town. We planned the first morning to go to the museum, but first had to convert some of our money to Euros. On the way to the bank, my daughter noticed a mannequin in a store window with an American paratrooper in a 101st Airborne Division uniform.

"Look, Pop. Let's go in and see what that's all about."

"Okay." That spur-of-the-moment decision changed the whole trip. I met Marco Kilian.

We entered what turned out to be a huge "warehouse" filled with World War II equipment—all kinds of military hardware, rifles and machine guns, bayonets and a jeep. The front part of the store had all other kinds of memorabilia, uniforms, books, maps, medals, all World War II oriented. As I approached the counter, a big man, Dutch veteran and paratrooper Marco Kilian, asked me if he could help me find something. I smiled and said no, that I had been here during the war; I was just looking around.

His eyes widened, and he said, "You were here during the war with the 101st Airborne Division?"

"Yes," I said. He came charging around the counter, and for a brief moment I thought he was going to attack me, but picked me up in a huge bear hug saying, "Oh Sir, you don't know how happy I am to see you. There are so few of you left and we wish to honor you all. What are your plans and how long will you stay in Bastogne?"

"We'll be here for three days, and I have no specific plans except to try to find the battlefields."

"What outfit did you serve with?"

"I was with H Company, 501st Regiment in the 101st Airborne Division."

"Oh Sir," he said. "We have all made a study of the war here for years. I can show you exactly where H Company was dug in during the battle."

I couldn't believe my good fortune. He asked my daughter and me to come back at one o'clock and that he and Johnny Bona (a Belgian tank commander) would take us in his car to the battlefields.

We returned at one o'clock, full of anticipation. As we were being driven out of town, I saw the church. "Marco, is that the church where we had the wounded laying on the floor during the battle?"

"Yes," he said, "we will visit that later."

About four miles out of town, near the little town of Mont, he stopped. We got out of the car. "Vincent," he said, "this is where H Company was dug in on both sides of the road. Did you tell me you were a machine gunner?"

"Yes," I said.

"Well, you were probably in that two-man foxhole over there," he said, pointing to a spot near the ridge line.

I was shocked. I looked over to where he was pointing, my mind in a turmoil trying to think back 65 years. It was difficult since there was no snow on the ground now and 65 years of growth had changed the landscape some, but gradually I began to flush as I pictured the fields covered with snow and the ridge where we were dug in becoming more familiar.

And then almost like a physical blow, it hit me right between the eyes. The noise came back, the terrible noise of artillery and mortars and the occasional cry of one of our boys who had been hit. I began to see all over again the first wave of Germans coming out of the woods, small doll-like figures that didn't look real. Tanks that looked like oversized toys making noises like popping firecrackers but which exploded into the sounds of hell when the shells reached us.

My mind's eye saw once more that first wave reaching approximately halfway across the open snow-covered fields toward us and suddenly stopping. I heard us crank rounds into the chambers of our machine guns and rifles, and wait for the lieutenant to give the word. "Not yet," he said.

We were busting. My heart must've been racing, pumping blood to my extremities because my hands were no longer cold on that gun. I could almost feel that same flush.

The shock was, that unknown to both the Germans and us, barbed wire fences ran across the fields, covered by the snow. The first wave just ran into them and got tangled. The second wave came on, and tried to help their buddies get off the fences. The advance stalled. When the third wave came up, now there were knots of men struggling in deep snow, and the Lieutenant gave the word.

The rest was in slow motion. We opened up with a vengeance. We fired and traversed across those groups and the snow turned red. I'm yelling again but no sound is coming out of my mouth. It was a machine gunner's "delight," and the bodies piled up. I couldn't recall any emotions other than a flushing of the face and what my friends told me later was a steady stream of cursing and yelling.

I was now a combat paratrooper worthy of my uniform and my wings. What a feeling! And it all came back. I broke down at the memory of the carnage.

My daughter took me aside and held me. "Marco," she said, "I think my Dad has seen enough for today, let's go back to town."

In the car on the way back, I asked Marco and Johnny if I could take them to lunch. When we stopped at the Leo Hotel dining room, I ordered three bottles of wine. I wanted to change the mood and get happy. We sure did! We ate and drank and laughed and talked loud. People were looking, but I didn't care. We started telling each other stories, and I told them the beer story.

As I got into the story, Johnny and Marco at the other side of the table began to look mildly shocked. They pointed fingers at me, "You, you, you were the G.I. who gave beer to the wounded during the war?"

"Yes."

"You were the G.I. who brought beer in his helmet to the wounded in the church during the battle?"

"Yeah."

"My dear Sir," they said, "don't you know you are famous in Europe?"

"What the hell are you talking about?"

"Waiter," they called. "Bring us four bottles of Airborne Beer."

In a few minutes the waiter came back with four bottles of beer on a tray and four ceramic bowls in the shape of the G.I. helmet. He served them. On the label of the bottle, there is a young paratrooper extending a helmet full of beer to his buddies.

And Marco and Johnny said, "No one thought that story was true, they thought it was just a rumor. But twenty years ago a Belgian brewer, right here in Bastogne, decided to dedicate a beer to this mythical G.I. And now," said Marco, "the guy is sitting in front of us. The story is real. What a coincidence."

Little did I know that for all these years, my "act of mercy" was being celebrated by beer drinkers all over Europe. I now carry a picture of Airborne Beer in my wallet to show people when I tell this story.

The next day, they took us to the church. This time I recognized everything almost immediately. My daughter and I entered the church. All of the blown out stained-glass windows had been replaced and the bare floor of the church was now covered with pews and benches. But the scene came back anyway—wounded men lying all over the floor wrapped in curtains, bed spreads, and whatever else we had been able to find in the way of blankets. No groaning or moaning, just a low sound of people conversing.

The beer story at this church is not funny now. There were a lot of bloodstains that had been cleaned up. My mind whirled and I got annoyed at myself at my lack of control. The tears flowed and I bowed my head. My daughter walked me to the back of the church.

As we were standing there and I was trying to compose myself, a little old lady approached, hobbling along with a cane, holding the hand of a small boy. She let go of the little boy's hand, and with her thumb wiped tears from my eyes and said, "Monsieur, Je comprend." (I understand).

Then the little boy stepped up and in very good English said, "Sir, thank you for our freedom." He stepped back and gave me a very smart British Army salute.

I lost even more of my cool. I shook his hand, kissed the old lady, and thanked them. I am now on an emotional roller coaster. What a defeat for a man who used to being so proud of his self-control. Age has its consequences.

I asked Marco to take me to the site of another grisly scene. During the war, when on a trip to headquarters, I had to walk past the courtyard to get to the church. At that time, the courtyard was filled with small jeep trailers containing the stiffened dead bodies of our boys stacked like cordwood and pathetically covered with a thin blanket. It couldn't be helped, because there was no way to bury the dead since the ground was frozen and no equipment for digging was available anyway. Still, it was sickening to see the yellowed arms and legs frozen solid, sticking out from under whatever was supposed to cover them.

When Marco took me to the courtyard this time, it was empty, just a flat cemented area. I held up fairly well.

We went back to town. I will never forget what happened when I asked Marco if I could take him and his wife to dinner that night in partial repayment for all his kindness to us. "Oh no," he said, "You and your daughter are coming to my house for dinner. My wife, Marion, is preparing a special Italian feast."

I was flabbergasted. A man who has known me for only two days, and his wife who hasn't even met me yet, have invited us to dinner. What magnificent people!

And what a dinner it was. The children were seated at a separate table, extremely well behaved, and courteously applauded when I played my harmonica for them. The Italian dinner at our table was superb with different kinds of wine served with different courses by the lovely Lady Marion, an exquisite hostess. How I loved everyone around me that night.

Before we left Bastogne, everyone there made me promise to return on December 16th for the annual celebration of the battle. They said that this 2009 celebration was of special significance since it was the 65th anniversary. The entire Belgian nation, realizing that the veterans still alive had to be in their mid-80s, might be seeing them for the last time. They said they would make sure there was a hotel room for me even though by now there wasn't a room available in all of Belgium, northern France, southern Germany, Holland, and Luxembourg. I found out later that this was not an exaggeration. I assured them that I would come.

Airborne beer

The tavern in which Vince first filled his helmet with beer
to bring "aid and comfort" to the wounded

24. "CELEBRITY?"

KATHY AND I WENT TO PARIS. TRY AS I MIGHT, I COULD NOT GET INTO THE tourist mode, thinking about the three days just past. I hoped I hadn't spoiled it for Kathy. Later, I rode home on the proverbial cloud nine, wondering how I was going to survive the two months until December 16.

The day finally arrived, and I did indeed wear a 101st Airborne pin prominently on my jacket lapel. It was amazing. While changing planes in New York City's LaGuardia Airport, the people waiting for the plane to Belgium began applauding. A young lady just walked right up to me and said, "Sir, are you a veteran of the Battle for Bastogne?"

When I said yes, she immediately called her mother up from her seat to take a picture of us. While that was happening, an elderly gentleman walked up to me, asked if I was going to the celebrations in Bastogne, and when I answered in the affirmative, told me that he was going there, too. He then just casually mentioned that he is Gen. Patton's grandson, and he too, wanted a picture with me. I felt like a celebrity, a feeling that was to be repeated many times over in the future, but I still consider undeserved. After all, we're talking about things that happened 65 years ago.

Arriving in Brussels, my friend Marco Kilian picked me up at the airport and drove me to Bastogne where I was greeted with enthusiasm by people like Carol Lentz and Christa de Champs who worked at the Museum and took me into their care. Meanwhile, Marco and Johnny Bona drove me about town to visit the monuments dedicated to the 101st Airborne. It was impressive!

I attended a ceremony in a building that I was told was made from all of the rubble gathered from the bombed out streets and buildings of Bastogne. The ceremony, where the four of us World War II veterans were the honored guests, was attended by the American ambassador, the

Dutch defense minister, the French ambassador, the Belgian minister for foreign affairs, NATO generals, and many U.S. Army personnel. I was not only impressed, I was awed. A lot of the speeches were in French, but enough were in English for me to understand what honors they were bestowing on us. I never felt so proud in my whole life when they asked us to stand up and applauded us soundly. What a moment.

However, it was a seemingly insignificant incident that led to more very pleasant memories. I met Kelly! Kelly Ann Sproul is a very pretty British singer with the most beautiful of soprano voices. She is known as the Sweetheart of the British Armed Forces. She travels everywhere in England and on the Continent singing World War II songs to veterans and their families. Everyone loves her. I first heard her sing in Bastogne at Marco's "Museum." She was on a small stage and I was sitting in a chair off to the side with two other veterans signing autographs.

Unbeknownst to me, her microphone cable passed under my chair. When I got up, I accidentally unplugged it. She was unaware that the non-reaction of the audience was caused by her singing into a dead mike. Her mother, Kim, who was her manager, quickly repaired the damage, and she went on.

After her performance, I quickly went up to apologize profusely. She took it all in stride and actually moved on to taking pictures with me and accepting my invitation to dinner for her, her mother, and her driver as a sort of "makeup." We had a wonderful dinner talking about all the places I had been in England before getting into the war. They were charming people, all three of them.

When it was time for me to leave, they asked Marco if they could ride with us to the airport. I was surprised to find them both in tears as we were saying goodbye. They kept repeating sincerely, "Vincent you must come to visit us in England; we would be honored." I believed they really meant it and I was sure of it after I returned home and they called me on the telephone, repeating the invitation. I agreed to go.

After I discovered that Kelly's birthday is March 24, Kim's is March 25, and mine is March 23, I decided that that would be a good time to visit. We would celebrate all three birthdays together. What a delightful visit that was. Kelly took me on one of her "gigs" and introduced me to some of the British veterans in the audience who then made me feel quite at home. Her grandmother and grandfather invited us to dinner, and I was happy to find that her grandfather liked to sing, as I did. We did a little sightseeing, but all too soon, it was time to leave. I told Kelly I hoped we would meet again in Bastogne in December. I went home with Kelly's beautiful music going around in my head.

It was now December, 2010. As I had hoped, Kelly was back at the Museum singing away. Once again I managed to embarrass her during her performance. (It is a miracle that this beautiful lady continued to tolerate my friendship.) I was in the audience with a group of paratroopers from other nations, when a big Polish paratrooper with a large, carefully groomed handlebar mustache, put his arm around me and said, "Feencenz, I hear all about you, you American paratrooper with hundred first Airborne Division in Bastogne during World War II. My father jump wiz First Polish Brigade in Holland."

He then thumped me on the back, pulled out a bottle of Johnny Walker Scotch from his kit bag and said, "I hear you like good whiskey." Well, what does a man do when handed a bottle of whiskey while standing among friends? He opens it, of course, and offers everyone a drink.

We got a little bit noisy.

Kelly was on the stage singing her World War II songs and we started singing the paratrooper song. We got so loud on the chorus, "gory, gory, what a hell of a way to die..." that the audience started singing with us. Ole Kelly, professional that she was, took it all in stride. She walked calmly over to us, handed us the microphone, and proceeded to lead the audience in the many stanzas of our raucous song. When it was over she graciously invited me up to the stage to sing with her. What a classy lady!

I later apologized to her, of course, and once again she said, "Oh Vince, it was loads of fun." I repeat, what a classy lady! She must not have been really mad at me because she invited me to come to England again, in March, at around our birthdays.

"I'd be delighted, young lady, I'd be delighted."

But the lasting impact of this gracious young woman was yet to come. I had told Marco that before I went home I wanted to visit the cemetery where my buddies from the battle of Bastogne were buried. There was a group of us, including Marco's son, Nino, Herb Souerth of Band of Brothers fame, Kelly, and Christa De Champs. It was a cold dark day when we arrived at the cemetery, and I began to shiver involuntarily. I asked them all to remain at the edge of the grass, and I approached the first cross. When I put my hand on it, intending to say a prayer, I fell apart. I sank to my knees imploring my comrades to forgive me for being such a coward and not returning to pay my respects for over 65 years.

It was then that Kelly and Christa picked me up and walked me slowly to the other end of the cemetery. Christa said something to me in French, and Kelly, with her eyes full of tears, said, "You're not a coward Vincent, you're a hero."

I had never seen such compassion in a woman's face. I looked up at her and said, "No Kelly, the heroes are the ones buried under the crosses. I got to go home and live a beautiful life with a wife and family."

And then Kelly said the most meaningful words ever uttered to me, which eased my guilt feelings. "Yes," she said, "but we honor them through you."

I felt as though a weight had been lifted from my shoulders. I often wondered why I was so reluctant to go back to the battlefields for 65 years. I think I now know. I didn't want to face those crosses. I promise to visit those crosses every year from now on for so long as I am alive.

On the way back in the car, as I was sitting somberly in the back, I heard Marco's eight-year-old son, Nino, saying something to me, but in Dutch. I asked his father to translate. Here is what he said, "I understand that you are sad. I would also be sad if my friends were dead. But don't cry. It is not your fault that they got killed but the fault of the Germans. And if you cannot visit them anymore, I will do that till I can't do it anymore."

I cannot tell you what affect those words had on my already twisted emotions. Can you imagine being comforted by an eight-year-old Dutch kid? Out of the mouths of babes....

Kelly Ann Sproul, the Sweetheart of the British Armed Forces

25. "MERRY OLD ENGLAND"

MY VISIT WITH KELLY AND HER FAMILY IN MARCH OF 2011 WAS PURE EN-
joyment. Not only did they take me to visit so many interesting places,
but they also helped me look for the Radbournes.

As you may recall in an earlier chapter, the Radbournes were the
family who took me in that early morning in England when I got drunk
at a pub and was left out in the alley by a bunch of British toughs. I had
an address for them and asked Kelly if we could look up their place in
Brighton. Upon finding the street, we discovered that there was no house
with the number of the address I had. When we spoke with a neighbor,
we were told that the house had taken a direct bomb hit during the war
and was completely demolished. The family wasn't in it at the time, but
they didn't know what happened to them.

Disappointed, I asked if there was a pub nearby that had been there
during the war. "Oh yes," they said. "The Fairfield Inn it's called."

Sure enough, when we went to look, there was the Fairfield Inn, the
pond, and the park at Queens Terrace. I sat on the bench and had Kelly
take my picture in the exact spot that I had sat 67 years ago as a bewildered
19-year-old soldier coming off a drunk. It was such a nostalgic moment,
I smile every time I see the picture.

We went to the newspaper in Brighton, the Argus, and I told them
the story. The editor thought it was interesting and asked permission
to print it. I said, "Yes of course, and would they please put my e-mail
address at the bottom and ask anyone who had any information about
the Radborne family to contact me." The newspaper printed a nice article
with my picture and my e-mail address.

Within two weeks after I returned home from England, I received
an e-mail from a Lynn Taylor who said she was May Radbourne's
granddaughter, and that May, as a five-year-old, remembered the day an
American G.I. came to their home and ate with them.

I was so happy. I e-mailed them back immediately and told them that on my way to Europe this summer, I would like to stop off in Brighton and take them to dinner. And so it was written and so it was done.

We had a delightful dinner, exchanged pictures, and I learned that most of the rest of the family had passed on. May was still going strong. I thanked her once again for the wonderful things that her family had done for me. We parted teary-eyed. I have some great pictures to remember her by.

In the summer of 2011, I brought Kelly to America to sing for American veterans. She was a great hit and received standing ovations everywhere we went. She was even interviewed by Dr. Mark De Pue, the director of the oral history program at the Abraham Lincoln Presidential Library and Museum. The interview is on the official website of the Presidential Library. Her story is a remarkable one as she talks about the World War II experiences of her grandparents who were in London during the blitz, and her meeting with Prince Charles.

In June, it was now time for the great adventure in Normandy.

May Radbourne and Vince reunited in England after 66 years

26. NORMANDY AND HOLLAND

BEFORE I LEFT BASTOGNE IN DECEMBER 2011, MARCO HAD AGREED TO plan a trip to Normandy for the June 6, 2012 annual celebration of the 101st Airborne Division jump on D-Day, and to Holland where the Division jumped in the Market Garden operation on September 17th. I had never been to either of these places and was very anxious to see them. Marco, who met me for the Radbourne dinner, had driven us from Brighton to Dover, then the ferry, and then to France.

What an experience seeing the actual fields where the boys jumped on D-Day. We visited a half a dozen museums, the St. Mere Eglise church with the parachute still hanging off the roof as seen in the movie *Band of Brothers*, and some of the new stained-glass windows now containing the Screaming Eagle as part of their design. We visited the fortifications at Utah Beach and I shuddered when I saw how those guns in the bunkers had every inch of the beaches covered and wondered how any of those boys in the landing crafts ever got up the beach to fight.

Though I did not jump in Normandy, everywhere I went I was treated with great courtesy and respect. A member of 101st Airborne Division can do no wrong in France. In all the years after the war when I was so angry so many times at the French government and its stormy relationship with the United States, I never dreamed that the French people still held the American people in such high esteem. Governments notwithstanding, everywhere we went, "Viva La France" was always followed by, "Viva La America." People to people.

We drove to Holland and an even more enthusiastic welcome, if that is possible. Again, though I did not participate in the Market Garden operation, I was treated like a returning hero. I visited the actual field where my regiment, the 501st, made its jump. I visited the bridges where so many of our men died taking them and holding them only to have to give them up to escape being trapped by the oncoming Germans when British armor failed to come up in time.

I have never been photographed so many times in my entire life.

In an interesting side trip, we visited a large Dutch farm, famous for its exploits during the war. The owner, whose son was now entertaining us, had built a false room in his barn, even changing the roof line, to escape detection. Here he hid downed Allied airmen, Jews, or underground escapees, waiting to be taken to a safe place by the Dutch underground. You have to admire the courage demonstrated here since the punishment for harboring fugitives of any kind was death to the entire family—men, women, and children.

When Market Garden failed and the Germans were coming back, this stubborn Dutch farmer dug deep trenches in his farm with his bulldozer and buried all of the equipment left there to deny their use to the Germans. His son showed us buried Bofors guns, tanks, a US Army Duck, and a German half-track troop carrier now partially uncovered. World War II produced many civilian heroes, as well as military ones!

I left Europe that summer a little awed by the heroics of so many people.

At Omaha Beach, Normandy, Vince marvels at how little damage Allied bombardment did to the fortifications.

Vince visits the new Waal River Bridge, Holland, September 2014

27. THE NEW HOME FRONT

MEANWHILE BACK ON THE HOME FRONT, MY FAMILY IS BLOSSOMING forth. In 2011, I became a great-grandfather for the second time with the birth of little Anna. In 2012, I became a great-grandfather for the third time with a great-grandson, Parker. They are all doing well and I get to see them quite often. I am also staying busy as Commander of the Veterans of Foreign Wars Post 8157, and Senior Vice-Commander of the American Legion Post 277.

I am asked to speak at various meetings of service clubs and other community groups. I am especially pleased when asked to speak to schoolchildren, especially high school students, some of whom may be interested in a military career. I write occasional articles for the local newspaper and do my best to stay well-informed on current events.

My new interest in military events and reunions begins to crowd my calendar, but I love it. To stay busy mentally and physically is to avoid Alzheimer's. I'm already devastated by its effects on my wife. God grant us a cure one of these days. It is mankind's most punishing disease.

In 2011, beginning to feel the financial pinch of so much traveling, I began thinking about a reverse mortgage, tapping the equity in my home for extra cash. I applied to AAG, having watched and been convinced by ex-Senator Fred Thompson's informative commercial.

Responding to my phone call, a man named Frank Malendrez adroitly explained the entire process and said he saw no problem with my getting the cash. About a week later, I received a surprising phone call from Frank saying I had been turned down. He said the underwriters (a bank) would not approve the loan, and without the underwriters approval AAG could do nothing.

"But Vince," he said, "it's not going to end here. I believe they are balking at your age and I'm not going to let them get away with it. A man with the finest credit ratings I've seen in a long time and a hero of

World War II (Frank's father was a World War II veteran) deserves every consideration. I'm going to work on this, even if I have to go right to the very top, and get you that loan."

Well, Frank did exactly what he said he was going to do. He called meetings of the top bosses, fought the bank, threatened to finance it himself, and got it approved. I was overjoyed with Frank's performance and thanked him and his father profusely. I also wrote the CEO of AAG a nice letter of approval of the actions of what I called, one of his most effective employees, Frank Malendrez and his assistant Stacy Kopekne. I've always felt that while most people are quick to write letters of complaint, they do not always write letters of commendation when called for. I do, and in this case I cannot believe the explosion of events that followed.

In the letter, I had said they could use this communication in any way they pleased, as it was all true and came from the heart. A week later I received a phone call from Frank. "Vincent, you don't know what you've done for us here at AAG. Your letter was transcribed and sent to all departments. Department heads called meetings, read your letter to their employees to show them the results of their efforts. The whole organization got a big boost in morale. May we use your letter in a brochure?"

"Of course," I said, "just let me see a copy after you make it."

"Okay Vince, they also asked me if you would mind sending them some pictures of yourself and your home, especially including some World War II artifacts." When I promised to do all that, he said, "And don't be surprised if you get a phone call from our Marketing Division." I had no idea what he was talking about but did what I said I would do.

A few weeks later, the brochure came out in full color featuring two full pages of my letter and pictures of me in uniform today and 65 years ago. By comparison, all the other endorsements in the brochure were 1/8 of the page in size. I was amazed and pleased to no end. I showed my copy to everyone. And then I got zonked with a phone call from the marketing department.

"Hello Vince, how would you like to come to California for three days, all-expenses-paid, and make a commercial for AAG with Fred Thompson?"

"Are you kidding me? I'd be delighted."

When they gave me the dates of September 28 to October 1, I hesitated. I was already committed to go to Belgium for the opening of the new 101st Airborne Division Museum and did not return from that trip until September 26. One day home and then off again? Ten seconds later; end of hesitation. Fix bayonets and charge!

"Of course, those days are just fine."

I told my whole family about it and they said they'd see to it that everything was in perfect order when I came back from Belgium and that there'd be no problem with the repacking and taking off the next day. My daughter, Kathy, is marvelous with those kinds of situations and can really make them work. I had no qualms. I now had two pleasant anticipations, Belgium and California.

When I arrived in Belgium in September for the opening of the 101st Airborne Museum, the weather was beautiful. Marco picked me up at the airport in Brussels and drove me to Bastogne. He spoke excitedly about the opening of the museum and said he couldn't wait to show me all the various exhibits they had garnered including, he said, a very prominent corner display case for my original World War II uniform and all the other artifacts I had loaned the museum. I too was a little excited.

And then there was the speech and the party! The ceremony for the official opening of the museum was a big deal affair. The American ambassador, the Dutch Foreign Minister, the Belgian defense minister, various other officials, and a bunch of NATO and American generals, plus other officers. There were only two of us World War II veterans of the 101st Airborne Division who fought in Bastogne—Herb Suerth of *Band of Brothers* fame and me. They asked us both to speak and we agreed. I was to be the last speaker.

The speeches of all the important officials went as per script, said all the proper things as per script, and drew the polite applause as do these occasions. Herb did his standard speech.

As last speaker, I decided to have some fun. I had had two scotches that afternoon and was in just the right mood to shake things up a bit. So after I said good evening to everyone, recognizing all the officials as per protocol, I suddenly burst out in barely recognizable French. A dull audience, most of whom were French-speaking, leaned forward.

What I said to them in the most horrible spoken French imaginable, was, while I did not know the French language, I did recall a handful of words from the French-English and English-French handbook that they had given us during the war. And I began to blurt out disjointed and unrelated French words and phrases which started the audience laughing. Like, "Where are the Germans? Do you have water? Where is a doctor? I am wounded. veit veit. You are pretty. Are you crazy? Do you have a toilet? I need a priest. Attention, the bombs are falling. Merde (shit) oh no, not that one, excuse me. Bonjour Mademoiselle, combien? (how much?) Oh M. vous se no correct. Vous non dir bonjour, combien. Vous dir, Good evening, Mademoiselle, how are you, what is your name? Voulez vouz promenadez avec moi, I am Vincent…combien?

Well, I had them going. The American ambassador did not know whether to shit or go blind, until he heard the roaring applause as I finished off, singing in French, "Ah le Petite Vin Blanc" (taught to me by a pretty French prostitute), knowing full well the words may have been naughty. Whatever!

Lately, during these insane moments, my motto has been, "I'm 88 years old, what the hell can they do to me."

Even the Generals' frowns turned into smiles, and to rub it in a little bit, I turned to them and saluted. And then the fun began.

The announcement at the ceremonies that there would be music, dancing, and snacks upstairs sent us all scurrying. When I appeared up there, I was surrounded by women asking if I danced. With two scotches and a third on the way, I can do anything. And so I said, "Of course."

When my legs started to go, I sat down. Whereupon, one of my four friends would come over to me and say, "Vince, this is Johnny Walker Blue Label, you have to taste this one."

"Okay."

The next time I sat down Marco came over, "Vince, this is Johnnie Walker Green Label, you got try this one."

"Okay."

Well, the inevitable happened, and I did not remember leaving the place. I was assured later that I did not embarrass anyone, including myself. I merely told Marco I felt a little weak and needed to go to bed.

I woke up the next morning in my motel room with a strange feeling. I went to look in the mirror and was horrified to see a big black eye, and my right fist hurt. I was beside myself!!!

You will not believe how I cursed at myself, "You stupid son of a bitch. You mean to tell me that at your age you're still getting involved in brawls like when you were 20? Or even worse, a jealous husband or boyfriend? You ruined everything. You made such a good speech, everybody liked you, and now, what are they going to think?"

I kept examining the black eye. I telephoned Marco; they all came up to my room.

"Marco, what the hell did I do last night?"

"You did nothing wrong, you were a perfect gentleman. You bowed to the women who danced with you, you kissed my wife's hand when you danced with her, you escorted them all back to their seats, and you did not trip or fall or anything the whole evening."

"But Marco, then how did I get this black eye?"

"Well," said Marco, "when you asked to be taken to your room, we did so and then tried to take your clothes off. You absolutely refused. You kept mumbling, 'I am perfectly capable of undressing myself, thank you.' You weren't, of course, but no matter how much we tried, you would not let us do it. So we just threw you on to the bed, and started to leave. As soon as we got out the door, we heard a loud thump, rushed back in, and there you were on the floor with your fist in your face down on the carpet. That's how you got your black-eye."

I was relieved to no end.

When I left for home the next day, I bought a pair of sunglasses to wear. Reality didn't dawn on me until I got back to the airport and my daughter, who was picking me up, expressed shock. "Pop, you've got a black eye. You didn't get into a fight in Bastogne did you? Pop, not at your age."

"No, No."

I told her the story, and said in a few days it would all be gone. "Yes," she said, "but you're supposed to go to California tomorrow to make a commercial." Oh my God!

As soon as I got home, I called AAG in California and told them I was still willing to come out there but that I had a black eye.

"A black eye," they said, "you've been fighting?"

"No, I ran into the proverbial door."

"No problem," they said, "we have makeup people who will take care of your black eye." And so it went.

I made the trip to California and was greeted warmly, and with big smiles. They didn't believe the "running into a door" story. They picked me up at the airport in a big black stretch limousine. They put me up in a luxury hotel in a suite just under the penthouse. And then they told me I had an open account at the bar and in the dining room. I had never experienced such luxury before and I prepared to enjoy it to the hilt.

The next day I met former Senator and presidential candidate, Fred Thompson. What a nice guy! He made me feel right at home with not one bit of tension while making the commercial.

When I got back to my hotel, I was informed by the maître d' that there was a special dinner-dance upstairs and that they had reserved a table for me and that I could invite anyone I wanted to enjoy the evening with. I asked Frank Melendez and his wife to have dinner with me. They accepted. We had a lovely dinner and then proceeded to the lounge to our reserved table. The band started playing and the dancing began. After the first number the bandleader made an announcement.

"Ladies and gentlemen, we are very fortunate tonight to have with us a true American hero (I begin to cringe). He is a Purple Heart veteran of the Battle of the Bulge. A paratrooper with the 101st Airborne Division. (I am trying to duck under the table.) Please stand, Vince." (Who the hell put out all that information?) As I rose, this whole upscale crowd, men in black suits and ties and slim, black-gowned women with blonde hair, stood up. The bandleader then led them all in singing God bless America *to me*.

I don't know how to behave at times like this. I'm overcome with emotion, yet I know I should say something in gratitude to acknowledge their kindness. I end up waving to the bandleader and sitting down, embarrassed, elated, feeling honored, feeling humble, and as always in situations like this, almost in tears thinking about my buddies under the crosses who never made it back to enjoy a life like mine.

A beautiful lady came up and asked me if I danced. I said "yes" and they proceeded to line up. Really and truly, I know what it sounds like, but it's true. Don't ask me why any lady would want to dance with an 87-year-old, but they did. And I have a bunch of beautiful pictures sent to me by my friend, Frank, to prove it.

I later found out that I was staying at one of the most expensive hotels in California, in Orange County, which is supposed to have more millionaires per square mile than any place in the country. No wonder the crowd looked upscale to me; they were. It made their tribute even more gratifying.

I left California with yet another wonderful experience in life. Being rich doesn't necessarily make you a snob.

Those people weren't.

Vince's WWII uniform and other war memorabilia on display at the 101st Airborne Museum, Bastogne, Belgium

28. THE INTERVIEWS

AT THIS TIME I MUST REINTRODUCE MARK DEPUE, THE PERSON LARGELY responsible for the initiation to what has now become a new life for me. It was 2010 and I was speaking to a church breakfast group in Springfield, Illinois. At the end of my talk, this distinguished looking gentleman came up to me and said, "I'm Mark DePue, Director of Oral History at the Abraham Lincoln Presidential Library. I was wondering if I might interview you for the record. You sound like you have had some interesting moments during World War II."

"Tell me about the program," I said.

"Gladly" he said, "but let's talk about it somewhere else, may I visit you at your home?"

"Certainly," I said. (I didn't understand why until later.)

We reached an accommodating time and date. Once at my house, and seeing more than just wartime pictures and memorabilia, he began asking me about my family and early childhood growing up in New York City during the Great Depression. He decided that I would be a good candidate for a videotaped interview for his oral history program. "Would I be willing to tell my story on videotape to be placed in the Abraham Lincoln Presidential Library and Museum archives?"

Before responding, I asked, "What happens to the material from the interview?"

He said it is eventually placed on the Internet for use by educators and other interested parties.

"Well now," I said, "I'm not so sure I want to do that. You mean to tell me that a guy like Michael Moore can take the information about me and my wartime buddies and twist it into an antiwar film clip or worse, a movie. No thanks, I won't interview on the record."

"Wait Vince," said Mark. "We can add a caveat that says no one may use this material without your written permission."

"Well that's different; under those circumstances, okay."

He arranged for a full two hour videotaping session at the Governor's special TV studio in Springfield. At the interview, skilled questioner that he was, and full, no-detail-left-out storyteller that I was, got us into trouble. At the end of the two hours, I hadn't even gotten out of high school. He asked me to come back for another two-hour session.

"Okay."

That one only got me into the war.

To make a long story short, there are now five two-hour videotaped sessions on file in the Abraham Lincoln Presidential Library and Museum's archives in the "Veterans Remember" section under Vincent J Speranza. The story of my life up to the present, laid bare.

And, he says, if I keep on having "adventures," he's going to bring me back. He calls it an "evolving" story.

Thank you, Mark.

29. PEARL HARBOR

IT'S DECEMBER 2011 AND IT'S TIME TO GET READY FOR MY TRIP TO PEARL Harbor, followed quickly by my annual visit to Bastogne. I'm really looking forward to the Pearl Harbor tour since I had heard so much about it from other veterans.

Before I even arrived in Hawaii, I began getting the royal treatment on the plane.

As I am walking through the first-class section of the plane, on the way to my coach seat, a man sitting in first class reaches up, shakes my hand and says, "Thank you for your service, young man."

I smile, return his handshake and move on. No sooner am I seated, when the stewardess walks up to me and says, "The gentleman in first-class says he wishes to exchange seats with you."

I smile and say, "Oh that's very nice of him but I can't do that, he paid a lot of extra money for that seat."

In a louder voice she says, and all the people around us are now listening, "He seems very insistent and really wants you to do it." Then looking at all the people around me, in a still louder voice she says, "And I think you ought to go for it."

"Go for it. Go for it," the people around me begin chanting. What pleasurable embarrassment. Sheepishly, I picked up my things and walked into first-class, thanking the gentleman profusely. The comfort and luxury of that trip all the way to Hawaii will not be forgotten. When we arrived, I sought him out to thank him again. All he wanted was a picture with me. I complied.

We were registered at the Royal Hawaiian Hotel from where the tour would begin. I knew no one in the group and began fumbling around with the papers, notices, schedules and other important tour information while waiting for the bus to take us to our first event. Noticing my not-too-well hidden silent cries for help, two young ladies, one named Shawn

Bury and the other Melanie Gustefson, sort of "took me in hand." For the rest of the trip, they guided, accompanied, did much of the legwork, and generally made me feel "well taken care of." What nice people there are in this world.

There were many memorable moments on this tour. Among them the visit to the Arizona and the heart wrenching story of the men trapped in the hull of the doomed ship as it turned over and sank. I wept as they read each name and rang a bell in memory.

We also visited the submarine, Bowfish, and while Shawn and I were walking across the deck, a strong wind blew my hat off into the sea. You cannot know what a disaster that was for me. My hat is special. It cannot be duplicated. It was custom made by Marco and on the inside was signed by Marco and his wife Marion during my first visit to Bastogne. My heart sank as it began to float past the bow of the ship.

At that moment, a tiny Japanese, or perhaps she was a Philippine woman came running across the deck with a long pole, net attached, and handed it to one of the men near the bow. The man made one long scoop and netted it just as it was about to disappear. Thank God for little women and "skilled scooper" men who can hit the target the first time and get it right. I have my hat today because of them, and will never put it in jeopardy like that again.

At another event we attended, we must have been late because the speech had already started when we arrived. You will not believe this, but the man speaking was the General in command of all American armed forces in the Pacific, who stopped in the middle of his speech upon seeing me enter the room, and said, "Ladies and gentlemen, I see that we are honored today to have a combat veteran of World War II with us." I continue to be amazed. I have a picture with him.

On another occasion, Shawn, Melanie, and I were walking toward the hotel when I continued to notice two men following us. I finally turned, held my brass knobbed cane in a defensive position, and said, "Who are you and what do you two guys want?"

"We're with the FBI," one said.

"CIA," the other one said.

"What do you want with us, we haven't done anything wrong?"

"No, No," they said, "we are just waiting for an opportunity to talk to you a little about World War II. We were at the meeting."

"Oh, that's okay then. Nothing official?"

"No. We're here on vacation, just heard about you at the meeting."

The ladies went back to the hotel and I joined the two men. We had a couple of drinks and went down to the beach to smoke cigars. We told stories half the night. And a good time was had by all.

Of course no trip can go by without my doing at least one silly thing; and this trip was no different. What happened was, the entertainment at one of our dinners was a Hawaiian hula dance show. Beautiful girls and handsome young men gracefully dancing on an outdoor stage. At the end of it, they challenged anyone in the audience to come up on stage and participate in an amateur hula dance. No one expected an 87-year-old. There were a lot of laughs as a whole bunch of young people and I did the hula. Yes, I had had my two scotches and was not embarrassed at all when I didn't win the contest.

At one of the last events, we met with four survivors of the December 7 attack at Pearl Harbor. I was fascinated by the stories of what they were doing exactly when the Japanese planes hit. I have seen a lot of movies about Pearl Harbor but nothing is as dramatic as listening to a man talk about actually watching the bombs drop out of the sky. And how about another man who had to dive off a burning ship into the sea full of burning oil?

Throughout all these events, I couldn't help but notice many tightlipped Japanese tourists who were there. How must they feel listening to all these things? What must they be thinking about as person after person tells the story of what the Japanese did that day? Did they feel shame, humiliation, sympathy? I wish I could've spoken to some of them. I never got the chance.

I came home from Pearl Harbor elated, better educated, happy to have made new friends, and a bit more disillusioned at what mankind is willing to do to his fellow man.

Vince reunites in Ohio with WWII re-enactors he met in Hawaii in 2014.

30. THE REUNIONS

IT WAS SOMETIME IN JUNE 2012. MY PHONE RANG, "YOU VINCE SPERANZA?"

"Yeah."

"You the Vince Speranza who was at Bastogne with the 101st Airborne Division?"

"Yeah."

"Where the hell you been, man, we're looking for you guys."

Me, somewhat annoyed, "Who the hell are you, talking to me like that?"

"Oh sorry, I didn't mean to sound like that. I'm Sergeant Major Bos, 101st Airborne, Fort Campbell, Kentucky. I heard about you from a friend of mine and can't believe you're not a member of the 101st Airborne Division Association. There are only a handful of you guys left and we want you all with us. Our Association has over 1,200 members, mostly Vietnam and later. You guys have an honored place with us, won't you please join?"

"Certainly," I said. "Send me the papers and I will fill them out and send them in."

"Okay Vince, and be sure to plan on coming to our August reunion. It'll be in Memphis, Tennessee, and Fort Campbell Kentucky. And again, sorry about my gruff introduction. Glad to have you aboard."

"Okay, looking forward to meeting you all in August."

The day I got to the August reunion, as I got off the shuttle and started walking toward the hotel where the reunion was being held, four big guys got off a bench and came walking toward me.

"You World War II, with the 101st in Bastogne?"

"Yeah."

Warm hugs all around. "Man, are we glad to see you. Who were you with?"

"H Company 501st."

They look at my ribbons. "Purple Heart and Bronze Star, eh, where is all the other stuff you should be wearing??

"I'm wearing enough."

"No you ain't."

They grabbed me under the arms and walked me over to a table in the trophy room and started pinning all kinds of badges on my hat and on my jacket. I try to protest a little, but they seem pretty determined so I just sat back and let them decorate me.

They then asked me if I smoked, I said, "A cigar or two per day."

So they took me to the smoking area. "Have your first one of the day and really tell us all about it."

What a greeting! What a bunch of guys! Within the first ten minutes, we were brothers.

That was my introduction to the 101st Airborne Division Association, one of the finest organizations I've ever had the privilege of joining. There was no need to feel anything but instant friendship everywhere you went. And what respect for your war record. For the first time in my life I felt I was talking to people that really understood everything I was saying about the war. Most of these men had been at war themselves. Though it wasn't World War II, combat is combat no matter where you engage in it, and there is a special affinity among those who experience it. Man, was I at home.

Very satisfying to me was that I finally heard the truth about the Vietnam War from the people who were there. Most of my information about that war and how it was fought was tainted by biased media coverage and politically correct pronouncements.

My instincts about that war were corroborated by my new friends. It's too much to go into here, but one thing for sure, the President of the United States, and all the American people need to rise as one and sincerely and deeply apologize to the men who fought so valiantly in that war but were treated so shabbily when they came home. God bless them all.

Then I met Billy Robbins. Instant buddy, like we'd known each other all of our lives. He kept telling me he was just a dumb-ass from Sharpsburg, North Carolina, who spent twenty years in the military with a lot of combat time in Vietnam. How easy it was to like Billy. He had a lot of good stories to tell and his self-deprecating humor was so enjoyable. He had his car there, and took me all over the place. He was really a good old country boy of the old-school. The kind that were generous, easy going, and gregarious; but when they had to be, were tough sons of bitches who took no-nonsense from anyone, especially the enemy.

He was a fellow machine gunner and we exchanged tips on how each of us had won the war single-handedly.

We were never late for the hospitality room, which opened at five o'clock. Music, fun, laughter, and free drinks. A disc jockey, there to provide entertainment, had to continue turning up the volume as we got happier and louder. I was sitting at a table with Billy, Rocky Ryan, Bob Press, and a few others whose names I did not know. The beer and scotch were flowing and I started singing softly as I am wont to do after a scotch or two.

I was shocked that none of them knew the airborne song. Pissed off, I stood up and hollered at everyone at my table to, "Sing the Airborne song, God dammit!"

They did. Nearby tables began to join us, and when we got to the chorus, "Gory, gory, what a hell of a way to die, he ain't gonna jump no more," half of the room, about 400 people, were singing with us.

The disc jockey came down off the stage, handed me the mic, and said, "Why the hell don't you guys come up on the stage if you are going to sing?"

I don't know if he thought perhaps he would be shaming us into silence, but if that's what he had in mind, did he make a mistake. I took the mic, waved to my boys at the table to join me, and we went up on the stage. Now we had the attention of the whole room and we sang every verse that I knew of the *Airborne Song*, and invented some new ones. It went over big and they asked us for a repeat performance the next two nights. We didn't do it; making fools of ourselves once was enough. But it was a lot of fun.

I am 87 years old at this time. How can an 87-year-old be having so much damn fun? I'm supposed to be bumbling around looking for a rocking chair. But it ain't happening. So be it. I will not look a gift horse in the mouth.

P.S. Somebody made a video tape of our "performance" and put it on YouTube. It's all over the internet.

Up until now, when I saw Billy Robbins, he was in silly, baggy worn-out looking shorts, knobby knees, and a work shirt. The last night, at the formal dinner, we were all asked to wear our uniforms. I was shocked that the tall, clean shaven, good-looking, dignified man in the beautiful uniform of a Lieutenant Colonel was Billy Robbins. What happened to the dumb-ass country boy? I couldn't believe my eyes. I almost saluted him. A Lieutenant Colonel. All I made in the service was PFC.

In addition, that night I found out that he had written two books and is starting on a third. I have since read the books and they are marvelous accounts of a young man growing up in rural and poverty-stricken North Carolina who then entered twenty years of government service fighting for our nation and people. My hat is off to you, Billy Robbins.

The daytime highlight of that reunion was going to Fort Campbell and watching the entire division in a parade celebrating its anniversary. All the big shots were in the reviewing stand, including General Petraeus who at one time commanded the 101st Airborne Division. What a beautiful sight to watch 10,000 of America's finest troops marching in perfect order across that field. But the big surprise was when they were within 50 yards of the reviewing stand, they stopped. There were seven of us World War II veterans on the sideline watching and applauding. The officer came over to us and told us to get in line in front of the Division; that we were to lead the Division past the reviewing stand.

What a thrill. The seven of us straightened our backs, including the one in the wheelchair, adjusted our uniforms, and left our canes behind. When the band started playing again, with great pride we marched, leading the Division past the reviewing stand. And then, a magic moment: General Petreaus, stood out in front of all the other VIPs, and *saluted us.*

I have never felt more pride in myself and in my country than I did at that moment. If only God had permitted my wife to share that moment with me, I would have gladly died immediately thereafter. God bless her and God bless America.

2012 on the homefront found me more and more in demand as a speaker. As my World War II stories began to spread, schools from the little towns around Auburn, like Girard, Divernon, Waverley, and Chatham invited me to speak. Other schools asked me to participate in their Veterans Day ceremonies, flag days, and any other excuse to invite a World War II veteran to address their students. Community groups and service organizations are also interested and I accommodate everyone that I possibly can. I am still in awe of all the interest and attention being given to things that I did seventy years ago, but I am determined to do what I can to share accurate information about those times.

As commander of the VFW, and Senior Vice-Commander of the American Legion, I find myself fighting a losing battle to increase the membership of those organizations. Most of the World War II veterans are now gone; and they are not being replaced by younger veterans. Our membership continues to dwindle and attendance at meetings is sparse. We have put on membership campaigns and drives to convince the younger veterans who we know are out there, to join and participate. We continue to point out that this is happening all over the country. It would be a terrible tragedy if veterans' voices were no longer heard in political circles. So far the response has been scanty, but we will not give up. It is vital that veterans' organizations remain strong and continue to participate in the political debate.

Also on the homefront, Eva, one of my granddaughters, finally presented us with a great-grandson. It gives the male side of the family one more recruit to counter the deluge of females that have descended upon us. Of course I love them all, but it's nice to know that there is a possible future paratrooper in the family. My great-granddaughter, Elora (age 3), can count in five languages and sing in three. As soon as she learns the paratroop song, we will sing a duet and record it for posterity. Hurry up, Elora, I don't have that much time left.

In March of 2012, I made my second trip to England. It was great reuniting with Kelly, her mom Kim, and Terry and Nan (Kelly's grandparents). This time Terry took me to visit some of the lesser-known World War II monuments in England. There was one memorial that almost broke my heart as it related the fate of twelve out-of-date Swordfish biplane torpedo bombers sent up against modern heavily armed German naval ships in the channel. It was all the British had to launch at that time. Not one of them returned.

Also, we really explored Dover and ate in some quaint restaurants. And a good time was had by all.

In the meantime, the search goes on for Joe Willis, the only World War II fox-hole buddy I have left, if he is still alive. I have searched all over the Internet, Army records, even death certificates in Tampa,

Florida, (his World War II address was 3808 Santiago St., Tampa, FL) but to no avail. My new buddy, Billy Robbins, has tried to find him and actually located the house on Santiago Street, visited it, and spoke to the present owners. No one had any knowledge of the Willis family. We found a record of his receipt of the Silver Star for action in Bastogne, but no other information about his whereabouts. I've tried the VA; they won't give out any information, something about privacy. How I wish I could find out anything about Joe Willis. He is my last link with people I actually fought with during the war.

Where are you Joe? I need to know what happened to you. I need to speak with your family and tell them about their father, the good times we had, and the bad times we suffered together. Please God, let someone turn up with information about a real war hero, Joseph A Willis.

I did find Louie Martins' family in Wrightsville, Georgia. Louie Martin was the guy in the barn who could not shoot the old cow. Louie is long since gone, but I did get to speak with his son and was able to tell the family about paratrooper Louie Martin, a first class fighting man, and his exploits in Bastogne and the rest of the war. They were grateful.

And I received another call which went something like this…

"Hello, Vince?"

"Yeah, Herb (Suereth, *Band of Brothers*), how are you doing?"

"I'm doing okay, Vince. I'm calling to invite you to the reunion of the *Band of Brothers* in Kansas City in October."

"October? That sounds great, I'd be most happy to attend, is anything special going on?"

"Yes, I hate to say it but I think this is going to be the last reunion. There are so few left able to travel, and the arrangements become more difficult every year, so we decided to wrap it up at Kansas City."

"Gee Herb; I'm sorry to hear that. I remember how some of them had difficulty the last time we were together. I'm glad you're giving me the opportunity to talk to some of those boys one more time about the jumps in Normandy and Holland."

"Okay Vince, see you there."

Meanwhile, during the month of September, my eye doctors had advised me to have my now "fully blossomed" cataracts removed. I was happy to do so since I was beginning to see gray areas while trying to read. What I didn't know, was that besides removing the cataracts, they would give me new eye lenses. While the entire procedure was tedious and complicated, the results were absolutely amazing. The new lenses improved my vision to where I no longer need eyeglasses for distance or watching TV. I now need only a pair of reading glasses. Colors are sharper and more distinct, and road signs have never been clearer. No more cataracts. What a wonderful modern miracle.

Although I drove myself alone to Kansas City (a six-hour drive), there was no shortage of helpful people once I got there. Katherine Archer (administrative assistant to Herb Suereth) and her sister, Elizabeth, sort of "took me in hand" and made sure that I was well taken care of. The visit itself was poignant and a little sad.

How I enjoyed being with my friend Marco, his wife Marion, and their two children, Nino and Dana, who also attended. In the happy moments we drank, sang, and told stories. In the sad moments we were saying things that sounded like goodbye. I went home sad but proud that these famous men in the *Band of Brothers* invited me to be with them though I was not a member.

"If we do not meet again, Brothers, good luck and Godspeed wherever you go and whatever you do. I am a better man for having known you."

31. MY FOXHOLE

I WAS NOW APPROACHING THE MOST IMPORTANT TRIP OF THE YEAR, MY visit to Bastogne in December 2012. I began to anticipate, get my finances in order, and made the decision to take my 19-year-old grandson, Will Sturgeon, with me. He and his mother (my daughter Kathy) were absolutely delighted at the prospect. From my perspective, I was making sure that at least one family member got to see and experience how the people of Belgium really feel about Americans and the 101st Airborne Division. It would corroborate all the stories I have told about these wonderful folks.

We arrived in Bastogne on December 14, having been picked up at the airport in Brussels by Marco. We stayed at the Leo Hotel again and were met by a pretty young lady, Mianne Irick whom I had met in Normandy the past June. She was friend to Herb Suereth's daughter who was also with us in Normandy. She's an American girl from Kansas City working in Germany on special writing projects which are then translated into nine languages. She drove all the way from Germany to spend the weekend with us and to witness the Bastogne celebrations. She also offered her help with the book I told her I was going to write. A delightful person and another good friend.

At Bastogne, we plunged into the action. At Johnny Bona's invitation, we visited the Belgian army compound just outside of town which houses a Belgian Tank Unit and a Museum. Will, Mianne, Marco and I were treated like visiting dignitaries.

On Saturday, Marco drove us out of town again to my foxhole. This time he had obtained the permission of the landowner for us to actually walk out to the foxhole instead of just viewing it from the road as before. This time I could actually say that 68 years ago I was at this exact spot, in this hole in the ground, with a machine gun, waiting for the first German attack. I turned to my grandson Will and uttered the famous phrase, "When I was your age m' boy, (68 years ago), I was right here in the middle of a war."

As I gazed out over that battlefield again, this time from the exact spot I had my machine gun set up, the scenes of that carnage began to emerge again. I imagined that I could almost hear the artillery, tank fire, heavy mortars, and machine gun bullets that were flying all about us that day. Once more I kind of choked up, and turned away. Two blessed Irishman who had asked to come with us that day approached me. One of them, Joe McCabe, said, "I have just the thing, Vince," and he pulled out a flask of good Irish whiskey. I repeat, God bless my Irish friends.

Marco then took out a few small plastic bags and placed some dirt from my foxhole in each of them. I had intended to take them home but found that I could not until they had been properly processed (Department of Agriculture rules about checking the soil for I don't know what). Marco promised me that he would get them properly processed and I could bring them home the next time I visited Belgium.

In a happier mood, we went back to town to participate in the Laying of the Wreath Ceremony at the town square. When they called my name, I had Will come with me and together, we placed the wreath, saluted the flag, did an about face and left. The wreath said, "God Bless the 101st Airborne Division—May the World Never Forget."

How proud I am.

In the ensuing parade, I marched up the street, was photographed dozens of times, and asked to sign all kinds of papers, pictures, even jackets and hats of people from the sidelines. What a feeling. My grandson was drinking all of this in, shaking his head, and taking pictures. He said he will never look at his grandfather in the same way as before. I hope it is the people and the events he has experienced here and not his grandfather that he is impressed with. I hope he tries to understand that the Belgian people's feelings run deep because an American parachute division entered their town and held off seven German divisions from re-enslaving them. They also realize the cost in American lives. And that's why they want their people never to forget the 101st Airborne Division.

My grandson was seeing it and feeling it instead of just reading about it in a book. I hope it sticks with him.

After the parade we dropped in on a warm, friendly, noisy tavern off the town square. The chatter dropped a little and applause broke out as we entered. I smiled and waved my cane. Handshaking and picture taking. Women of all ages kissing me on both cheeks and thanking me for their freedom. Fathers thrusting their sons forward for pictures. We drank, laughed, sang, and I played the harmonica. Do you wonder why I like to go back to Bastogne?

The next day, I asked Marco to take me to the church to show my grandson where the beer story took place. I had intended to keep it lighthearted, but too many vivid memories frustrated my intent. When I started pointing out to Will where the wounded were lying on the floor wrapped in curtains and bed spreads, I started to get emotional again. When we got outside to the courtyard and the scene came back to me of all those dead troopers, frozen solid, stacked like cord wood in little trailers with an absurd little blanket on top of them, I lost it again. But I stayed in there until I explained fully to him what it meant to be in a war where you are surrounded and cannot even take your wounded to a field hospital in the rear, nor even bury your dead out of sight. It can be a little unnerving.

It was no better when I asked Marco to drive us to the cemetery for me to pay my respects to my fallen comrades. I knew exactly what was going to happen, I tried to steel myself against it since it would be especially embarrassing in front of my grandson, but I knew I had to do it anyway. And it came to pass.

I walked out by myself, kneeled at the first of the white crosses and tried to pray. I didn't get very far before the sobs came. I bowed my head as low as I could, trying to hide my weakness. I didn't do very well. Marco and Will came and got me and walked me to the car. I did okay on the way home.

Sometimes I wonder why I keep going back to revive those images. Why don't I just stay away from them and try to forget. Then I stop wondering and know why. It's because I do not want to forget them now. I want to remember them, talk about them, pass them on to as many people as I can before I leave this earth to make up for the 65 years of neglect when I spoke nothing of the war.

Our people should know and remember. I'm going to do what I can to help.

Vince and grandson Will at Vince's foxhole outside Bastogne

*Vince and grandson Will in front of
a refurbished US WWII Tank in Belgium*

32. MORE REUNIONS

I NO SOONER ARRIVED HOME FROM BASTOGNE IN DECEMBER, WHEN I began planning for the next venture, in February, the 101st Airborne "Snowbird" reunion in Tampa, Florida. I had some real work to do because they informed me that at the last night's special dinner, the World War II veterans were expected to come in their original uniforms and medals. When I complained that mine no longer fit me, the answer was "get it fixed." I proceeded to look for a seamstress who could alter my uniform to fit. I found one in Springfield in a shop called Sun Sewing and took my uniform in. What a nice job she did and in plenty of time for the February reunion. I packed it carefully, realizing that it and all the ribbons and medals and buttons on it were 70 years old.

The pure enjoyment of the occasion began immediately upon my arrival. My good friend Billy Robbins "took me in hand" again and ran me through the registration and the other procedures necessary to the event. We then went to the hospitality room where "beverages" were available from early on. He then told me that we needed to get a table in the corner to "operate from." I didn't know what he was talking about, but went along.

What I soon found out was that they had planned a little ceremony for me. They asked me to stand up and then one of them began to read a proclamation that Billy Robbins had put together. They gave me a notebook with pictures, comments, and a brief history of my service. They presented me with a leather vest, the back of which read "Vinnie, World War II paratrooper, H Company 501st, 101st Airborne Division" all in big yellow letters for all to see. When asked to speak, I could hardly get the words of thanks and gratitude out. What a heartwarming rendition of friendship and respect.

I shall not forget it. (My head size used to be 7 1/4—I don't know what it is now.)

And then a guy named Russell approached me, and said, "Vince, I'm tired of watching you with those el-cheapo cigars you smoke. I have gone to great lengths to find some real cigars which we will now go out and enjoy."

True to his word, he handed out big, long, expensive-looking cigars to everyone, and we went outside to the chairs near the pool and lit up. The clouds of smoke that billowed up must've looked like a fire had started. We did a little singing, drinking, and harmonica playing before we went back in. Another pleasant two hours with magnificent friends.

I then heard an electrifying statement. There was going to be a parachute jump tomorrow.

"Marco, would they let me jump?"

"I don't know, Vince, let's go ask."

We hurried to the registration desk. "I'm Vince Speranza. I want to get in on the jump."

"Do you have all your paperwork in order?"

"What paperwork?"

"Copies of your discharge papers or other evidence that you have had parachute training, the notices about that went out weeks ago."

"I didn't know anything about it. If I call my daughter and have her fax a copy of my discharge papers which indicate that I went to parachute school, would that be sufficient?"

"Probably."

I proceeded to place a frantic number of phone calls to my daughter but, to no avail.

"Listen guys, isn't it obvious that I had parachute training? Good God, I served with the 101st Airborne Division during the war."

"Sorry Vince, but the rules are pretty clear, hard and fast. We must have the proper written documents. I tell you what we will do though, I'll have the secretary call the U.S. Army records division and ask if they will fax us a copy of your discharge papers."

"Fantastic; please do."

She did, but no dice. The Army would not fax any documents (too easy to fabricate). They would only send them in the mail. Bitterly disappointed, I resigned myself to defeat. How terrible I felt that the high hopes I held briefly for once more enjoying that magnificent experience of a parachute jump were dashed. I had already imagined standing in the door, feeling the rush of wind past the plane, watching for the green light, and then stepping out into the void. You drop 32 feet, the static line pulls your chute out, the prop blast fills it, and you swing out under it. Blue sky and quiet while you check your canopy. The gods are cruel.

However, they told me that the August reunion of the 101st Airborne in Portland, Oregon would also sponsor a jump and that if I had the proper paperwork, I could be included. You can be sure that as soon as I got home, I would be properly prepared for August.

When it was time for the Saturday night dinner, I proudly donned my old World War II uniform. It was still a little tight but fit well enough. Command Sergeant Major Grippe came over and congratulated me for looking like "a real paratrooper from the old days."

The pièce de résistance, was that they allowed me to be one of the after dinner speakers. I told them the beer story. In the write-up afterwards they called it, "the war story of all war stories." (Head size…)

I still can't believe what has happened to me in the past three years since my first visit back to Bastogne in 2009 after a hiatus of 65 years. What a world I'm living in, my only regret being that my wonderful wife cannot share it with me.

As I was saying goodbye to all my friends, Marco asked me what I was going to do when I returned home.

"Settle down to an old man's pace for a change and devote more time to the homefront. My next trip is not until June to the 501st PIR reunion in Albany, New York. That gives me a few months for rest and rehabilitation."

They laughed and said, "We'll give you three days after you get home." They were right.

Vince riding with 501st Paratroopers on a helicopter jump at their reunion in Alaska.

Dr. Govaerts's son (left) finds Vincent with Johnny Bona (center) and thanks him for his kindness to his family during the siege of Bastogne

33. AND THE BEAT GOES ON

IT'S 2013 AND I'VE BEEN INVITED TO THE 501ST PIR REUNION IN ALBANY, NY. I knew no one there, but was soon introduced to many friendly faces. One of the other World War II veterans came up to me and said, "You Vince?"

"Yeah," I said extending my hand. He shook it and said, "Heard you were with H Company 501."

"Yeah."

"So was I, Name's Ed. I was a medic with H Company, assigned to the third platoon."

"No kidding, I was in the third platoon, were you with us in Bastogne?"

"Yeah all the way; patched up a lot of you guys in that one."

"Were you with us after we broke out of Bastogne and got into that fight near Heuffilize?"

"Yeah, that one was a bitch."

"Then you must be the guy who, when I got hit, helped Steve (Pentek) pull me into that hole and pumped me full of morphine."

"I guess so; I was the only medic there with the third platoon."

"Well I'll be damned; just before I went under, I heard you say to the guys who were trying to get me on that jeep stretcher, 'don't shake this one up too much, he's got a piece of shrapnel under the eye brow and it might be touching his brain.'"

I remember so clearly, to this day, my final thought was: "Great, now I'll be a fucken vegetable." I was sent to a British hospital where, happily, they removed the sliver of shrapnel with no problem.

"I know it's 70 years late, Ed, but thanks again, anyway."

I also met a woman named Tedi. She was a fellow harmonica player and she and I had a great time playing all the old songs with harmony. All in all, another good reunion, with lots of nice people.

It was now June of 2013 and I headed to Normandy for another interesting adventure. Marco Kilian and Herb Souerth were my companions and both had been there before. They showed me the landing fields where the 501st jumped on D-Day. They took me to Utah Beach where I got a good look at those formidable fortifications and once again wondered how any of our boys got up those beaches. Met some more great people and vowed to come back.

August 2013, and I attended the 101st Airborne Division Association Reunion in Portland, Oregon. Another bunch of great guys and gals. This time, when they gave me the usual five minutes at the end of the program, I read a poem that I had written the previous week entitled "The Machine Gun Kid." (see appendix)

It describes my first day of combat in Bastogne. It was well received. It's the first poem I ever wrote, and I cannot believe that even today, when I read that poem, I get emotional. It was printed up in the next issue of the Screaming Eagle magazine. Subsequently, it appeared on the Internet.

It was now September 2013 and the whirl-wind continued. I was in Holland celebrating the September 17, 1944 Market Garden operation. How sadly impressed I was at viewing the bridges where so many men died to take them, only to have to give them up as the operation failed. I also visited the landing fields where the 501st jumped. I stayed at the home of Marco and Marion Kilian during this visit. I got to visit and speak at a Dutch school. I was so impressed at the courtesy, intelligent questions, and general demeanor of its students. I believe it was on the high school level, but they appeared and sounded more like college students to me.

We attended a series of ceremonies so sincere and impressive they made me realize again and again that the Dutch people have never forgotten us Americans of World War II.

It was October now and I had again been invited to attend the Curtis High School class of 1963 reunion in New York City—the 50th this time. The same group I met with five years ago, only now my "kids" are 68 years old. A delightful dinner, an opportunity to speak to them, and wonderful memories reactivated. In addition, an unexpected bonus in the knowledge that my former student, General Altshuler, would accompany me on my visit to Bastogne in December.

November brought a fantastic trip to Alaska.

I was speaking with a young new paratrooper at Fort Campbell. When I asked him where he had taken his jump training, he surprised me a little by saying he did not have jump training. It was only then that I recalled and fully realized that the 101st Airborne Division was no longer jumping. They were Air Assault—helicopter boys. What a disappointment. I asked the whereabouts of my old regiment, the 501st, since it did not appear to be at Fort Campbell. He told me there was only one battalion of the 501st left and it was in Alaska, but they were still jumpers! Still real paratroopers. I vowed to somehow go see them.

This situation was resolved so simply when I received an email inviting me to the 501's Geronimo Ball in Anchorage in November. I was delighted and made preparations to visit them, accompanied by my granddaughter, Emily Yeager, as caregiver. You cannot believe the reception we received.

We were met at the plane by two officers, Lieutenant Connor Flatherty and Lieutenant Matt Carstensen, XO, with a big bouquet of flowers for Emily. They drove us to our hotel, saw us safely registered and set for the evening before they left, promising to pick us up in the morning for the visit to the Base.

They did. And then the fun began. They introduced us to the commanding officer, Colonel Toby Magsig, and gave us a written schedule of events that they hoped we would be willing to adopt. It included interviews with various people like Justin Connoher, the public relations man, and various television and newspaper people who were there to record our visit. How complimentary they all were.

And then a bombshell! Hanging on the wall of their Headquarters Building in a glass case was a large Nazi banner given to the 501st years ago, with all kinds of signatures on it from the third battalion of the 501st. Guess whose name was on it? Right there with some of my buddies like Steve Pentek and Joe Willis, was Private VJ Speranza, signed in 1945. Everyone took pictures of me pointing to those signatures. Echoes from the past.

They took me down to the weapons room and showed me what the modern paratrooper has when he goes into combat today. A far cry from my .30 caliber light machine gun during World War II.

And then, joy of all joys, they put some warm clothing on me and let me accompany a parachute jump out of helicopters. Four times I went up and watched those great young men and women jump out of those helicopters, static lines pulling open their chutes, and sailing gracefully down into the snow. How I pined and pined to be allowed to jump with them, but the answer was "no." I so enjoyed that action, having never been up in a helicopter before.

I was then interviewed by the TV stations and asked to read my poem "The Machine Gun Kid" for the public relations boys.

Saturday night, as a guest speaker, they cheered as I called them "My 501 boys" the last of the jumpers. I told them some stories and a little bit about the battle for Bastogne.

It's hard to believe but, after my speech, they lined up four abreast for more than two hours, to shake hands with Emily and me and take pictures. Fortified with a Scotch that Emily, now and then, supplied me, I had no trouble responding to these great people. I never felt so good in my entire life. I had come home!

About a week after I had returned from the trip, I received in the mail a magnificent plaque—2' x 3', beautiful dark rosewood frame, and a wonderful display of paratroop wings, insignia, a static line, and other medals against a blue background. What a beautiful thing to have hanging on my wall. I almost tear up every time I look at it.

And now for the big one. It was December and I got ready to go to Bastogne, this time accompanied by General Altshuler.

While I was grateful for the receptions I received in Normandy and Holland, I always felt a little non-deserving because I did not jump in Normandy or Holland. But in Bastogne, I was at home, because I was right in the middle of that fight.

Oh how enthusiastically the people greeted us. Everywhere we went, in the company of Sebastian and Carol Lentz, we were warmly received. Since Marco couldn't be there, he arranged for Sebastian and Carol to take over my schedule. We went to the 101st Airborne Museum where Hans and his wife entertained us grandly and then permitted me to visit their latest innovation.

They had set up a room in the basement of the Museum to give people the experience of being in a bomb attack. It was uncanny. The room was dark and forbidding looking. Then you heard the planes come over and the entire room shook with the thunderous explosion of bombs and shells. It was almost for-real to me. I almost relived those days of 1944 in Bastogne under heavy bombardment.

The next day, Saturday, they said would be a little more lighthearted.

They took me to a nightclub where, after a Scotch or two, I sang the paratroop song with the band backing me, and everyone in the audience singing. Fun, fun, but Sunday was the real surprise. All they told us was to report to the Bastogne Tank Compound outside of town. When we arrived, there were people all over the place, all with flags and cameras, cheering. There were eleven Sherman tanks with motors running.

The third tank (symbolic of General Patton sitting in the third tank when he entered Bastogne in 1944) had a ladder up against it and two burly Belgian soldiers holding it. They indicated that I was to get up in the tank. With their help and Carol Lentz's, I did. And then the entire tank column, with me standing in that third tank like the general, paraded around the compound three times to the cheers of everyone. What a moment! What an experience! What a display of warmth and friendship! It almost seemed too much for an 89-year-old. I thanked them all again and again.

I left Bastogne in tears as I hugged all my friends. Hopefully I will see them again to continue to express my gratitude for making an old man feel so good.

It is 2014 and I am dying to get to the 101st Airborne reunion in Tampa, Florida, because I am scheduled to make a jump! Can you imagine, I'm going to hit the silk one more time.

I make sure all my papers are in order, that I have signed all the forms, and I have paid all the fees. I have exercised regularly and feel perfectly fit to make that jump. That Saturday morning, having reported to the airfield, I was asked to pass the test of a PLF (parachute landing fall). I passed with flying colors; in fact, all the younger men applauded my PLF. I was assigned a chute and a jump position.

I could not believe it was really going to happen. Then the word came down, "Jump canceled. The ceiling is too low, but tomorrow morning the weather is going to be just fine. Everyone report back 7:00 AM."

I'm disappointed but happy; it's going to happen anyway tomorrow morning. That night a phone call comes in to our jump master. "Everyone can jump tomorrow except Speranza. There is a new FAA regulation that says no one over 80 years of age can jump."

I explode! What kind of horse shit is this? Who the hell is the FAA to tell me whether I can jump or not jump out of an airplane if I pass all the tests and sign all the release documents? I protest, but to no avail. No jump for me.

However, I have an ace in the hole! Last summer when I was in Holland, Marco introduced me to a tough bunch of boys from the Dutch Marines. Their commanding officer, a major, took a shine to me and said, "If they don't let you jump in the States, you come back to Holland and I'll get you a jump, and out of a C47, too."

First chance I got after Tampa, I called Marco and asked him to get in touch with the Dutch officer and tell him I did not get to jump in the States, could I hold him to his promise. Marco did, and the major did. Screw the FAA, I'll jump in Holland.

I was so annoyed I almost didn't read my second poem when they gave me my five minutes at the end of the program. I relented. It's called "The Ubiquitous K Ration and it's Aftermath"(see appendix). I wrote this one because I was informed that my "Machine Gun Kid" poem had brought some of the ladies to tears. I wished to change the mood this time. It too, was well received.

Except for the failed jump, it was a good reunion. I continue to meet interesting people.

Vince and MG (R) Buz Altshuler at one of the many memorials to the 101st and 82nd Airborne Divisions in Bastogne

Some of the four generations of women in my life.
Left to right: Daughter Kathy; granddaughter Eva; wife, Iva;
granddaughter Emilie; great granddaughter Elora; and granddaughter Ella.

Vince, honorary tank commander, Bastogne, 2014

Airborne beer

34. THE GREAT DILEMMA

I NOW ACKNOWLEDGE THE GREAT DILEMMA! HOW DO I END MY LIFE STORY when it is not over yet?

My friend, Mark DePue, has said that my story is "an evolving one." When I look at my schedule for this year, I can't help but notice that I have an out-of-town or overseas commitment every month until January 2015. Some months have two trips. So what great adventures will I still experience? What interesting people will I still meet? What further conclusions will I still draw from my continued "wanderings?" And most important of all, will I get to make my parachute jump some place?

The answer to those questions will just have to wait. I am determined to publish now while my mental faculties are still intact.

The decision to publish this book triggers a small alarm. I feel as though I am walking through the public square discarding layers of protective clothing one piece at a time until I stand naked and vulnerable as my life story is revealed to all.

So be it! I have done my best to tell this story honestly, accurately, and without additions, omissions, or exaggerations.

DID I DO IT RIGHT?
YOU BE THE JUDGE!

VINCENT J SPERANZA

H Company 501st PIR, 101st Airborne Division
Bastogne, Battle of the Bulge, Combat Infantryman's Badge

Bronze Star, Purple Heart,
Knight of the French Legion of Honor

Soldier, Sailor, Schoolteacher, Union Organizer,
Scout Master, Community Volunteer

Husband, Father, Grandfather, Great Grandfather,
Veteran, and Patriot

APPENDIX

A KID WITH A MACHINE GUN

It was December of nineteen and forty four
The eighteenth to be exact,
When the hungry, tired soldiers did pour
From off the trucks with their packs
And told to dig a hole in the frozen ground.

And It was cold cold cold.

The wind blew through their summer clothes
And feet froze through and through,
But these were Paratroopers all
And given a job to do.
No weather was going to stop these boys.

And we waited waited waited

We checked and checked and checked our guns
Our fingers stiff and sore,
The enemy was near we knew,
Get ready, sight that bore.
Put a round in the chamber, and click it home.

And we stamped and stamped and stamped our feet.

The experienced calmly lit a butt
And cupped it in their hand,
The young kid with the machine gun
Just hoped that he could stand.
They all gave him the "thumbs" up, "you'll make it little man."

And you force a smile while your mouth runs dry.

The fog and mist begin to rise
Daylight comes at last,
Stirrings from the other side
Artillery comes whizzing past.
Not yet, says the Lieutenant, not yet, not yet.

And our fingers were sticking to the triggers.

And then the sound we dreaded most
The clank of treads and wheel,
The eighty-eight grinds to a halt
And the tanks belch red-hot steel.
Fear begins to clutch the heart.

And you shiver a little and blame the cold.

The enemy starts across the field
White snow capes frustrate our aim,
"Lieutenant, Goddamit, they're coming on"
Are we just playing a game?
Not yet Not yet Not yet, says he.

And the wind blows swirls and swirls of snow.

The machinegun Kid hears not the din
Waiting only for word or plan,
His thoughts exploding again and again
Would the Kid become a man?
He sets his sights at 400 yards and squints through the peep hole.

And the figures get larger as they come on and on.

Now! Now! Now! the command, hoarsely thru the noise,
My gun erupts , I grin and shout, And curse and curse and curse.
My fear is gone replaced by joy
As I watch the figures fall.

VINCENT J. SPERANZA

Joy ? I don't know, The snow turns red with blood.

And the enemy Falters, Stops, and Turns Back.

No victory cries or shouts of glee as we all turn around
And view the bodies of OUR boys lying upon the ground.
Oh the cost the cost, of that days' work, lies heavily on the brow,
The mighty Airborne One O One is less in numbers now.
But we stopped them cold ; Though odds of 7to1,No Nazi Boot Ever
Entered Bastogne.

And the Machine Gun Kid had indeed become a MAN.

We the living seek not the glory,
Only realization of our terrible losses,
We ask for honor, respect and prayers for
The brave men 'neath rows of crosses.

Vincent J Speranza
"H" Co. 501 PIR
101st Airborne Div.
Bastogne 1944-45

THE UBIQITUS "K" RATION
AND ITS AFTERMATH
- or -
THE MACHINEGUN KID
RIDES AGAIN

The military mind, who invented the box, known famously as K RATION,
  Ought be sent to Hades, and forced to eat, 10,000 with a passion.
The outer covering so tough with wax, defied cold hands or a bayonet,
  It practically took a hand grenade, and a concentrated mindset.

  Its contents were three cigarettes, three biscuits hard as nails,
  A packet of coffee called Nescafé, and candy that tasted like snails
But the prize was a little round tin, different for each meal of the day,
Breakfast- chopped eggs, lunch was cheese, supper was pork that looked gray.
  greasy greasy greasy

  Now if they could be heated, they weren't so bad,
      but fires were taboo in battle,
    Eaten in sequence might avoid disaster,
      since greasy food that causes the rattle,
  Is bound up by the cheese, of the savior lunch packet; relief;
      but a temporary stall.
'Cause at night, that sneaky gray pork, proceeded to undo it all.

  In Bastogne we were down to two rations per day, and unfortunately
      the cheese units went
          missing.

All we got were a bunch of the greasy ones,
and the rumble became a hissing,
As foxhole after foxhole emptied its residents,
shedding their clothes as they ran,
Natures demand could not be ignored;
but not in your foxhole man !

Saving the best for last, I deliberately left out, in my description of the contents of the K ration, the small piece of brown paper, about the size of your hand, included as toilet paper. But cold stiff fingers and the very thin paper, caused unbelievable catastrophes. If you think bombs bullets and snow are the only miseries of war, you are mistaken. Taking off your clothes in zero weather, relieving yourself with inadequate wiping material, and no way to wash anything, add immeasurably to the terror of battle.

Early one night, while waiting for darkness,
to cover our trip to the wood,
We'd eaten two greasy units that day,
and anyone would have understood,
Our groans and moans when the Lieut.
Said, "get up, we're changing position."
"Lieut. you're taking a hell of a chance,
you have men here all in transition,
About to become immobilized by explosion."

2.

We walk and walk, and try our best, the pressure beginning to peak,
"Lieut. Lieut. we have got to stop, our defenses are getting weak."
He pays no heed to our pitiful pleas until a field and hay stack appear.
Then grudgingly he says," OK, Let it Go, and lets get out of here."

AND THEN THE UNTHINKABLE!
A German flare arcs across the sky.

Daylight descends on the fields below
And voices are heard to cry, Oh No,

Hit the Dirt! Hit the Dirt! Hit the Dirt! The Command,
But trousers at ankle height demand,
"What manner of order can this be?"
The rain of the mortar shells say, Don't wait to see,

The men dive forward, though some fall back,
Lower parts of anatomy hit the snow with a whack,
Oh the cold, the shock, the indignity, and pain
As 98.6 meets 12 below zero.

As the flare dies away and recedes in the night
The men slowly rise , full of anger and freight.
For the question the question, most difficult to bare,
Was, Checking it carefully, Do I still have a Pair?

The Machine Gun Kid, being late to disrobe,
laughed and laughed at the discomfort of others
But as shrapnel landed around his earlobe
He soon joined the plight of his brothers.

But Ladies and Gentlemen; without attempts at rhyme, the sight of that sea of white asses, glistening in moonlit snow, like lighted candles on a birthday cake, will never be erased from my mind.

Fortunately, no one was injured that night
Though many of us came close, but in fact,
In spite of the Nazis determined best efforts,
Our Manhood was still intact.

SILAS (NOT HIS REAL NAME)

He sits inside the darkened room
Its window sill cracked and worn.
The ashtray overflows with butts
His clothes are ragged and torn
He needs a shave and a haircut too
His teeth look bad, but what can he do?

The house behind this body of pain
Is in need of much repair.
Overflowed baskets show his disdain
For letters that would strip him bare
"Where did you serve, and when and how?"

The telephone rings, he does not answer
"I don't need no help from nobody."

There was a time when that paunchy body
Was tall and big and strong
He ate up the miles on the daily runs
And excelled at firing guns
The army he served thought he was great
And sent him over to fight.
He did the job, was wounded twice
But survived to see the light.

Silas came home to stings and jeers
Not understanding his country's plight.
Vietnam they said, was not a Just War
And his Silver Star was not right.

Were his days and nights in the steaming jungle
Nothing more than a great big Government bungle?

Understandably then, the stress and strain
Made it difficult for him to readjust.
So Silas withdrew within himself
And his brain began to rust.
Trouble with jobs, he started to drink,
Drugs followed soon thereafter.

The manly body began to shrink
Taut muscles went soft and slack.
He took any job that he could find
To earn enough money for smack.

His former character finally took hold
And he threw off the offending habits.
But no family, no friends to help him out
They had all disappeared like rabbits.

No matter, "I don't need no help from nobody."

So Silas lives from day to day
A grizzled old man now dying
But the fierceness in his bloodshot eyes
Denies him his need for crying.
"I don't need no help" is still his creed

should someone come to his door,
But the Angels in heaven would condemn us all
If we didn't try some more.

For tis man was a warrior, ready to lay down his life, for all of his
countrymen

We should seek him out, with the resources we waste, on Criminal
Behavior
And despite his resistance, bring soothing balm, and help him meet his
Savior.

AN OLD PARATROOPER'S LAMENT

We all must have a secret dream. A secret hearts' desire,
A burning hope of something that, will set the soul on fire.
The day arrives, when hopes and dreams, can no longer lie in wait,
'Cause now old age is the determinant, of every person's fate.

So shyly you begin to talk, to family and to friends
Who think you're crazy, seeing the world, through a colored, distorted, lens
"Go home old man and take your pills, you know you're over the hump."
But in your heart, you know you want, to make JUST ONE MORE
JUMP.

To stand once more in the open door, your static line intact,
To hear C47 engines roar, and the jumpmaster at your back.
To feel the rushing flow of air as he loudly hollers "Go",
And you leap into the endless void, shouting "Geronimo."

A jerk, a pull, and the prop blast makes, your parachute blossom forth.
Oh faithful canopy of mine, sustain me 'tween heaven and earth.
Great faith have I that you will land me, safely on the ground,
And I will smile and smirk and jeer, at the doubters all around.

Unfortunately my lament remains, an unfulfilled desire,
The Government unilaterally decides, the situation is much too dire.

They sternly forbid and old man's wish, though he passed all tests just fine,
The problem they said, GET IT THROUGH YOUR HEAD, YOU'RE
FREEKING 89.

Now who the hell are they to say, "He ain't gonna jump no more"
It seems to me, that last great fight, was in nineteen forty-four,
It was all about freedom, for everyone, not just a European or two,
Americans were also free to live their lives anew.

So how about this old grey head, who wishes only to prove,
That a good American Paratrooper can, will make the mountain move (a
little).

THE AMERICAN SOLDIER

He asks for nothing, except our support
For his family in case he dies.
He may not always meet our goals,
But we know damned well he tries.

America has always produced such men,
And today they are still involved,
In keeping the enemy from our doors,
Though the problems seem never solved.

So when you meet one face to face,
Don't compromise on a great big smile.
And tell him that you really know,
He's walking the extra mile.

MARINERS HARBOR, S.I. N.Y.C.

by Vincent J Speranza, his brother.

REVEREND CLERGY, FAMILY, AND GOOD FRIENDS OF JOE SPERANZA. I'M
Vince Speranza, 78 and younger brother of Joe, next in line on the male
side of the Speranza family and probably the closest to Joe as the family
was growing up.

I'm here to honor Joe.

I ask rhetorically, " what is the measure of a good man?" The response
probably differs with different cultures but, in ours, I would accept, "One
who has had a positive influence on his own life, the life of his family, and
the lives of his friends and neighbors." This would automatically make
him a very positive influence on his community and his Country. By this
measure, Joe was a Good Man and, in my book , a Great Man.

You younger family members must have probably noticed that in his
later years Joe seemed A little "testier", perhaps more fiercely independent,
giving even more gratuitous advice, and generally more willing to talk
about his own experiences and virtues than ever before. And oh the
stories, again and again, the same ones which seemed to indicate that
his generation did it all and you "kids" don't have a clue as to what life
is all about. Was this a thinly disguised braggadocio or do old folks have
a change of character? Was Joe unique in this regard or do all old folks
get this way ? I assure you of the latter, for, what you are witnessing in
advanced age, is Man fighting his last struggle to convince himself and
all others that his life had meaning. He wishes to consider himself more
than just a nanosecond in the eons of time : More than a speck of cosmic
dust in the vast reaches of the universe ; More than just a tiny pinpoint
of light, easily extinguished, in the endless Cosmos. For you see, Mans'
greatest fear is not death, but death unrecognized for what he was or
what he accomplished in his lifetime. Young people caring for the elderly
need be patient and forgiving, for the condition reaches us all eventually.

If I were to characterize Joes' younger days, I would have to say that Joe was never really "young". You see, my father was one of those really lucky people who was able to hang on to a job during the entire Great Depression when half of America was unemployed. Unfortunately however, the job was in Flushing Meadows, Queens, which meant that Pop had to travel 2and ½ hours to work every day and 2 and ½ hours back - 6 days a week. He left home before we kids were up and returned late in the evening, exhausted, prepared only to eat a simple meal and then to bed. This meant that the day-to-day operation of the family and the responsibility for the rest of the children (8 of us) rested on the broad, magnificent shoulders of 14 year old " Joey." I don't think Joe ever thought about it, didn't feel it was an assignment, didn't ever consider any alternative . He just automatically and instinctively took the full responsibility for the care of the family in Pops' absence. Justice was meted out swiftly but fairly. Punishment was rare but effective. But kindness, protection, care and laughter were always in abundance. The evidence of the success of his guidance is everywhere in the accomplishments of all of we younger children of the family. With older sister Nancy as Minister of Internal Affairs, and Joe as Minister Without Portfolio for Foreign Affairs, the family prospered. Momma may have made the basic decisions but Joe was her very effective Executive Assistant.

I recall so many incidents illustrative of Joes' sterling character. I remember a Saturday morning when I would be pulled from my warm bed by Joe at 4:30 AM and told to get dressed. Joe then asked Momma for 50 cents, tied our little wagon to his bicycle, put me on the cross bar, and then pedaled 6 miles from where we lived in Port Richmond to the truck farms in Bulls Head. There he waited until the big buyers from the stores made their choices. Then he would buy 50 cents worth of leftover vegetables like carrots, tomatoes celery and broccoli, place them in the wagon and pedal home. There he would repackage them into attractive bundles tied with spaghetti string. He next took me in the house (I was 7, Joe was 14 ,) dressed me in clean shorts, white shirt with Buster Brown collar, combed my hair and shined my shoes. As we pulled our wagon through the neighborhood I would be instructed. " Vinnie, go up to that house, smile, and say, Lady, wouldn't you like to buy this nice bunch of carrots? Only 5 cents? He made me rehearse it until I had just the right amount of pathos in my voice and then told me to go do it. Oh how it worked. Before we had gotten half way through the neighborhood, Joe had turned the 50 cents into 5 dollars and proudly plunked it on the table when we arrived home. How Momma would smile. After all, 5 dollars from the kids when Pop was only bringing home 8 dollars a week was really something.

I remember other Saturdays when Joe would place 2 large cans of water in the wagon, some digging tools, and a piece of oilcloth to kneel on. Then he pedaled us to the cemetery on Forest Avenue where worshippers were paying their respects. Again I would be dressed and instructed, "take your hat off, no smiles, and look sad." Inevitably, the mourners would motion us to the grave and ask us to freshen the soil and water the flowers. We made a dime here, a nickel there, and by the end of the day, Joe was able to proudly plunk 2 or more dollars down on the kitchen table.

On still other Saturday mornings I recall Joe getting me out of bed and announcing, we're going crabbing." Placing his nets and lines on the bicycle, me on the crossbar, he would pedal the 8 miles to Fresh Kills Bridge where we crabbed all day. How I loved it. Bringing home a burlap sack half full of "Jersey Blue" crabs was another occasion for Momma to smile since it meant that crabs would be used to flavor the Sunday spaghetti sauce eliminating the expenditure for meat.

Joe was also an inventor of sorts. He hated to spend money for anything he thought you should be able to make for yourself. He made a "hotdog cooker" with nails sticking out of a board and an electric current going through them. The hotdogs impaled on them were supposed to cook rapidly that way. Unfortunately he used galvanized nails and the family thought it had been poisoned that night.

He also made a malted milk machine which I thought was marvelous except that the milkshake tasted slightly of machine oil which dripped down the shaft.

Joe actually made the first radio set in our house, a crystal set grounded to the hot water heater in the kitchen. How proud he was to place the earphones on our heads so that we could hear the faint music of a local radio station.

Our first TV set was a kit that Joe put together at a fraction of the cost of a "store bought" one.

But my warmest memories were of the loving care he gave me. Like the time he took me by the hand and walked me to the Palace Theater in Port Richmond to see a movie. The lobby was extremely crowded and when the crowd began to close in on us, Joe wildly elbowed a small clearing around us, lifted me high in the air and shouted, "be careful, I've got a little kid here."

I could go on and on. I won't; except to say that his adult accomplishments are legendary , going from a lowly electrician's helper to Chief Electrical Inspector for the entire city of New York.

So we say goodbye now to Joe. Dutiful son to his parents, wonderful husband to his beloved Millie, loving father to his children Ralph and Geraldine and proud grandfather to Michael, Joey, and Stephan.

Godspeed Joe on your journey to Heaven, for that is surely where you are going. You will be sorely missed here by us all.

And GOD, Please receive my brother into your care with kindness— for he deserves the best that Heaven has to offer.

So Long Joe
God Bless You And Keep You
Brother Vinnie

GENERAL EISENHOWER'S SPEECH TO THE 101ST AIRBORNE DIVISION

IT IS A GREAT HONOR FOR ME TO BE HERE TODAY TO TAKE PART IN A CER-
emony unique in American history. Never before has a full division been
cited by the War Department, in the name of the President, for gallantry
in action. This day marks the beginning of a new tradition in the American Army. With that tradition, therefore, will always be associated the
name of the 101st Airborne Division and of Bastogne.

Yet you men, because you are soldiers of proved valor and of experience,
would be the last to claim that you are the bravest and the best. All
the way from where the Marines are fighting on Iwo Jima through the
Philippines and southeast Asia, on through the Mediterranean, and
along this great front and on the Russian frontiers, are going forward
day-by-day those battles, sustained by the valor of you and other Allied
units, that are beating this enemy to his knees. They are proving once and
for all that dictatorship cannot produce better soldiers than can aroused
democracy. In many of these actions are units that have performed with
unexcelled brilliance. So far as I know, there may be many among you
that would not rate Bastogne as your bitterest battle. Yet, it is entirely
fitting and appropriate that you should be cited for that particular battle.

It happened to be one of those occasions when the position itself was
of the utmost importance to Allied forces. You in reserve were hurried
forward and told to hold that position. All the elements of drama – battle
drama – were there. You were cut off, surrounded. Only valor, complete
self-confidence in yourselves and in your leaders, a knowledge that you
were well trained, and only the determination to win could sustain
soldiers under these conditions. You were given a marvelous opportunity
and you met every test. You have become a fitting symbol on which the

United States, all the citizens of the United Nations, can say to their soldiers today. "We are proud of you" as it is my great privilege to say to you here today, to the 101st Division and all its attached units, "I am awfully proud of you."

With this great honor goes also a certain responsibility. Just as you are the beginning of a new tradition, you must realize, each of you, that from now on the spotlight will beat on you with particular brilliance. Whenever you say you are a soldier of the 101st Division, everybody, whether it is on the street in the city or on the front lines, will expect unusual conduct of you. I know that you will meet every test of the future like you met it at Bastogne.

Good luck and God be with you.

To The Paratroopers of the 501st Parachute Infantry, 101st Airborne Division — a first class fighting organization — with best wishes

Dwight D Eisenhower

AMERICAN AND FOREIGN CITATIONS

501ST PARACHUTE INFANTRY REGIMENT
FRANCE
DECISION NUMBER 367

The President of the Provisional Government of the French Republic: Cites to the Order of the Army

501st Parachute Infantry Regiment

A splendid airborne unit which gave proof of extraordinary heroism in the course of the Normandy landing operations on 6 to 8 June 1944. It parachuted before dawn on the assault beach on 6 June and in spite of all sorts of difficulties, succeeded in regrouping. Attacked by important forces with violent fire, it nevertheless occupied positions of strategic importance for the landing of friendly troops. This action open the way to La Douve and the Carentan road for the assault troops. In this way it greatly contributed to the first phase of the liberation of France.

This citation includes the award of the Croix de Guerre with palm.

Paris 22 July 1946
Signed: Bidault

501ST PARACHUTE INFANTRY REGIMENT
HOLLAND
NATIONAL DECREE OF THE NETHERLANDS
MINISTER OF WAR, DATED 20 SEPTEMBER 1945,
SECTION AI, SECRET NO. P 203

The Minister of War

Considering, that the outstanding performance of duty of the 101st Airborne Division, United States Army during the airborne operations and the ensuing fighting action in the southern part of the Netherlands in the period from 17 September to 28 November 1944 has greatly contributed to the liberation of that part of the country;

Considering also, that it is desirable for each member of the division who took part in the aforesaid operations, to possess a lasting memento of this glorious struggle;

DECREES:

That each member of the personnel of the 101st Airborne Division, United States Army, who took part in the operations in the southern part of the Netherlands in the period of 17 September to 28 November 1944, is authorized to wear the Orange Lanyard, as laid down in article 123 g of the clothing regulations 1944 of the Royal Netherlands Army.

Capt.Rodilas

J.G.v.d.Glas.

501st Parachute Infantry Regiment
Belgium

The Minister of National Defense has the honor to inform the Commanding General of the 101st Airborne Division that, by order of No. 1196 of His Royal Highness The Prince Regent, dated 22 October 1945, the 101st Airborne Division and attached units comprised of 501 Parachute Infantry are cited twice in the Order of the Day of the Belgian Army with the award of THE FOURRAGERE 1940

The 101st Airborne Division, U.S. Army, landing by parachute, glider, and assault craft on the coast of France, 6 June 1944, was one of the first units to attack the enemy in the campaign that was to liberate Europe from German domination. It was necessary for small groups to battle fiercely in many places in order that they might reach and unite at the assembly point. Many casualties were inflicted upon the enemy and many casualties were sustained by the Division while it subdued enemy strong points, attacked and held vital communication centers, bridges and observation posts. The success with which these missions were accomplished hindered the enemy from using reinforcements which could have caused the failure of the landing of the VII Corps, which later participated in the liberation of Belgium.

BATTLE HONORS

Battle honors ... In the name of the President of the United States as public evidence of deserved honor and distinction ... The 501st Parachute Infantry Regiment is cited for extraordinary heroism and outstanding performance of duty in action in the initial assault on the northern coast of Normandy, France. In the early morning of 6 June 1944, the 501st Parachute Infantry Regiment descended by parachute in the swamps in the vicinity of Carentan, France. Widely dispersed during the descent, the regiment suffered heavy casualties from determined enemy resistance. Small groups assembled whenever possible and fought their way to the assembly area. En route many enemy strong points and pillboxes were liquidated through acts of gallantry and disregard of self by individuals of the regiment. According to the plans, the bridges and crossings of the Douve River were seized and held in the face of heavy enemy fire. This prevented the enemy from bringing up reinforcements to prevent the beach landing of the assault forces of the VII Corps. The determination and gallantry of the 501st Parachute Infantry Regiment protected the south flank of the VII Corps, enabling a rapid inland advance of the assault troops and assured the establishment of the Allied beachhead in France.

The following unit is cited by the War Department in the name of the President of the United States as public evidence of deserved honor and distinction. The citation reads as follows:

101st Airborne Division with the following attached units 501st Parachute Infantry Regiment

These units distinguished themselves in combat against powerful and aggressive enemy forces composed of elements of eight German divisions during the period from 18 to 27 December 1944 by extraordinary heroism and gallantry in defense of the key communications center of Bastogne, Belgium. Essential to a large-scale exploitation of his breakthrough into Belgium and Northern Luxembourg, the enemy attempted to seize Bastogne by attacking constantly and savagely with the best of his armor and infantry. Without benefit of prepared defenses, facing almost overwhelming odds and with very limited and fast dwindling supplies, these units maintained a high combat morale and an impenetrable defense despite extremely heavy bombing, intense artillery fire, and constant attack from infantry and armor on all sides of their completely cut off and encircled position. This masterful and grimly determined defense denied the enemy even momentary success in an operation for which he paid dearly in men and matériel, and eventually morale. The outstanding courage, resourcefulness, and undaunted determination of this gallant force are in keeping with the highest traditions of the service.

War Department General Orders No. 17, 1945

THE LAST LETTER

Dec. 7, 1945

Dear Mom,

Well, I've moved again.
I am now at Camp Oklahoma
City, just outside of Reims
France. When I got back from
England, I found that my
old outfit had been broken
up and I was transferred to
the 82nd Airborne Division.
From here we will soon
sail to England and from
England to the U.S. We are
being processed and issued
clothing and equipment to

go home with. Today is
the last day for mailing letters
so this is the _last letter_ you'll
receive from me. Don't write
me any more because I
won't receive them. You'll know
when I'm home by watching
the papers for the arrival of the
82nd Airborne Division in N.Y.
We are going to march in a big
parade in N.Y as soon as we
land. It will be sometime
in early January, ~~maybe~~ maybe
the 5th or the 6th I'm not sure.
As soon as ~~the~~ you hear the
the 82nd had a parade

in N.Y. then you know that
I'm in the states and will be
home in a few days. Now listen
carefully Mom, — all my mail
will be sent to my home
address, I won't receive
anymore over here. So any
mail that you get addressed to
me, save for me, Don't
open any of them or don't send
them to me, just keep them
there at home until I get
there. Also there will be a
package addressed to you
from Scotland, Don't
open it, I want to

do it when I arrive.
I'm leaving it to Nancy to
take care of those things for me
my mail & package. When I
get home I'll show you why
I don't want it touched until
I get there. Now don't forget,
Don't write me any more and
don't expect any more letters from
me — this is the last one.
Watch for the 82nd Airborne in N.Y.
I'll be home early in January.
So until I see you all at home,
so long, a Merry Christmas
and God Bless All of You.
        Your loving son
            Vinnie